Poor Will's Almanack
and Horoscope in Nature

for 2019

by
Bill Felker

The Sun rises and the Sun goes down and hurries to the place where it rises. The wind blows to the south and goes around to the north; round and round goes the wind, And on its circuits the wind returns.

Quoheleth

Copyright 2018 by Bill Felker

Published by the Green Thrush Press
Box 431, Yellow Springs, Ohio

Printed in the United States of America
Charleston, SC – July 2018

All rights reserved, including the right to reproduce this book or portions thereof in any form whatsoever.

ISBN-13-978-1722969363

ISBN-10: 1722969369

The Monthly *Almanack* Sections Contain:

Seasonal Quotation
Gregorian Calendar
Essay by Bill Felker
Astronomical Data: The Sun
Phases of the Moon
The Planets, The Stars, The Shooting Stars
The Seasonal Affective Disorder Index
Peak Activity Times for Creatures
Meteorology: Cold Fronts and Lunar Influence
Best Lunar Planting Times
Calendar of Feast Days for Gardeners and Homesteaders
Almanack Literature: Reader Stories

The Months of the Year

January	Page 21
February	Page 41
March	Page 59
April	Page 79
May	Page 99
June	Page 117
July	Page 133
August	Page 149
September	Page 169
October	Page 187
November	Page 205
December	Page 223
Valediction for the Year	Page 241
About Bill Felker	Page 243

Bill Felker

Introduction to Using *Poor Will's Almanack*

THE ALMANACK HOROSCOPE IN NATURE (TIME WATCHING)

As above, so below.

The word horoscope comes from two Greek words, *hora*, which means hour or time, and *skopos*, which means observer. The time observer is a horoscoper, and for the horoscoper who watches the seasons, an "almanack horoscope" can offer a useful guide to the galaxy as well as to one's own neighborhood.

In *The Emerald Tablet,* an ancient text by Hermes Trismegistus, the author attempts to explain the astrological mysteries of the cosmos. The work contains the phrase: "As above, so below."

Indeed the land does reflect the sky above it, and the Earth watcher can create constellations and stories no less than the traditional astrologer. For the horoscoper, the landscape is rich with lessons and with possibilities for alignments and predictions.

By focusing on events in nature, the time watcher not only observes how the weather and the movement of the Sun, Moon, stars and planets are connected to the seasons but also how events on

Earth reflect what happens in the sky and how all of these events can be related to human emotions.

ALMANACK WEATHER

Like any Scripture, Earth's Matter is subject to our Doubt. But to the one who listens closely to its Cadence, it reveals the sweet hidden Truth.

Reginald Johnson, *On the Shapes of Leaves*, 1697

The weather estimates in this *Almanack* are the are based on my charts of fractal weather patterns I made between 1978 and 2018. Readers of my weekly and monthly columns throughout the United States have used these estimates successfully since 1984.

My interest in the weather began in 1972 with the gift of a barometer. My wife, Jeanie, gave the instrument to me when I was succumbing to the stress of school in Knoxville, Tennessee, and it became not only an escape from intense academic work, but the first step on the road to a different kind of awareness about the world.

From the start, I was never content just to watch the barometric needle. I had to record its movement. I was fascinated by the alchemy of my charts and graphs that turned rain and Sun into visible patterns, symbols like notes on a sheet of music.

From my graphs of barometric pressure, I saw that major high-pressure systems move across the United States an average of once every five to six days, and approximately 80 significant highs cross the Mississippi River in a year. Fronts move more quickly in the colder months. October through March can bring up to eight waves of high pressure every 30 days. The warmer months between April and September are more likely to have six or fewer fronts; June, July and August sometimes only produce two or three significant systems.

The weather records also showed that each week of the year was no less distinct than each month. In addition, the study of weekly weather revealed pivotal times in the year: days or groups of days during which the seasons obviously shifted.

A short apprenticeship told me when important changes would occur and what kind of weather would take place on most any day. That information was expressed in the language of odds and percentages, and it was surprisingly accurate. Taking into consideration the consistency of certain patterns in the past, I could make fairly successful estimates about the likelihood of the repetition of such patterns in the future. The pulse of the world was steadier than I had ever imagined.

The more I learned about the natural cycles in and around my home in southwestern Ohio, the more I found applicable to the world beyond the village limits. The microclimate in which I immersed myself gradually became a key to the extended environment; the part unlocked the whole. My backyard gnomon that measured the movement of the Sun along the ecliptic also measured my relationship to every other place on Earth.

Weather and Fractal Patterns

Like almanackers and other horoscopers, some Chaos Theory physicists also look at patterns in nature, and they have come up with notions that support the ancient use of barometric patterning in tracking and predicting likely weather scenarios. (Chaos Theory is concerned, in part, with discovering order in patterns or systems that previously were thought to be completely random.)

In the late 1970s, an IBM research scientist named Benoit Mandelbrot looked at fluctuations in all kinds of phenomena, from the stock market to cloud formations. He came to the conclusion that these very different occurrences were related to one another, and that they revealed an underlying force that pervaded every aspect of life on Earth.

In each of the events he studied, Mandelbrot found "self-similar" systems, which he called fractals. It is probably easier to picture a fractal than to define it. Imagine an electrocardiograph analysis of your heartbeat. The ups and downs are arranged on the paper in an orderly fashion, but never at exactly the same intervals. Or picture a month or two of a graph of the Dow Jones averages. That's a fractal pattern.

Although a weather graph of temperature or barometric pressure may chart very different activities and show much greater variability than the electrocardiograph record. Mandelbrot would posit that all such fractal records are showing us a life principle, not unlike a yin-yang law, which underlies not only weather, stocks and heartbeats but almost everything from the shape of ferns and fiords to the filigree in lungs and leaves.

That there is a relationship between heart rhythms, barometric rhythms, temperature rhythms, the patterns of clouds, the stock market and even the shape of frost on the windshield of my truck in winter, is apparently not a matter of too much debate, at least among some Chaos Theory physicists. All of the systems mentioned can be charted as fractals, and a visual analysis of their designs reveals their broad similarity.

Graphs of barometric pressure reveal many of the topographical patterns of the seasons. For example, August's barometric configurations are slow and gentle like low, rolling dunes. Heat waves show up as wide plateaus. Thunderstorms are sharp, shallow troughs in the mellow waves of the atmospheric landscape.

At the close of Late Summer, the year begins its ascent to the steep cliffs of December. Throughout Early Fall, the barometric waves become stronger; the high-pressure peaks become taller; the lows are deeper, with almost every valley bringing rain or snow.

Middle Fall is the rough piedmont of another country, stripping foliage, putting buds into dormancy, burning away the undergrowth and revealing the dark hillsides. At the end of Late Fall,

December's great range of cold and snow fills the horizon. Beyond it lies another immense upland, the frigid, high plateau of Deep Winter in which nothing ever seems to grow or change until the ground crumbles and gives way, shattered by thaws, and time tumbles down into the sudden, stormy gorge of March.

During the Middle Ages, the Doctrine of Signatures held that the shape of a plant's leaf or root held the key to its medicinal use. Thus, the hepatica leaf, reminiscent of the shape of a human liver, indicated its application in the treatment of liver ailments.

Modern fractal theory posits a not so dissimilar view that patterns observed in such diverse phenomena as the stock market and barometric pressure might not only hold the key to understanding the rhythm but also the ultimate cause and meaning of those phenomena. Some analysts believe that fractals could explain the source not only of our personal decisions but also of the outside forces that influence them.

Until more information is accumulated and analyzed, however, anyone with a barometer or a thermometer can keep his or her finger on the pulse of the world. Simple records of fractals provide easily accessed and interpreted estimates of future events, estimates (but not predictions) that can be applied with considerable accuracy. More important than forecasts, however, is the feel and the rhythm of the planet that awareness of climate and weather can bring.

Certainly, I can agree with science writer Marc

Ward, who states in his text *Beyond Chaos*, that fractal theory in its broadest sense improves our deepest sense of the universe.

"Nothing can detract from the fact that a common cadence has been heard and all of us can listen to it if we choose," Ward says. "We share a thrilling pulse with a huge part of this world, the solar system and the universe at large. We belong here. We know our place. We know our place and we are home."

THE TWELVE SEASONS OF THE YEAR
in *Poor Will's Almanack for 2019*

Seasons are defined by their events rather than by months or solar markers in *Poor Will's Almanack for 2019*.

The following sub-seasons divide the traditional four seasons into periods that are characterized by what happens in them rather than by dates. Many of these periods occur during different months in different locations, but they are all defined by their fauna, flora and weather.

For example, Early Spring arrives between middle February and late March in the East, Lower Midwest and Middle Atlantic States. This season usually begins several weeks earlier in the South, and up to four to six weeks later in the Northern states. The states of the West, Southwest and the Northwest may follow this sequence of seasons, but the markers for seasonal change are often quite different from those mentioned in this *Almanack*.

***

Early Winter: This first of the year's twelve seasons contains about six major cold fronts, and it lasts from around the first week of December until about ten days after solstice. Early Winter's nights are the longest of the year, and its cloud cover is the most intense everywhere in the United States.

Deep Winter: This season also has six significant cold waves, and it lasts from the start of the New Year up until the last week of January. Average temperatures in this season are the lowest of the year. Few visible changes in fauna and flora take place above the 30th Parallel.

Late Winter: This period contains five to six cold fronts and lasts from late January through middle February. Average temperatures start to rise throughout the nation now. Late Winter brings significant changes in flora and fauna throughout the South.

Early Spring: A relatively long season of eight to ten major fronts, Early Spring lasts from mid-February through the end of March along the 40th Parallel. Although the weather is usually raw, the first trees and flowers bloom, and migratory activity increases.

Middle Spring: A brief but dramatic season containing about four fronts, Middle Spring lasts throughout most of April (March in the South, May in the North). The first major bloom of wildflowers and domestic bulbs occurs. The weather becomes much milder, and the farm and garden year gets underway.

Late Spring: This season has five gentle fronts and stretches until the end of May. Most spring woodland flowers complete their bloom during this time, and almost all the trees leaf out. Frost season ends, and gardeners sow tender garden flowers and vegetables. Farmers put in all the corn and soybeans.

Early Summer: Containing four or five fronts (at least one of them followed by the first heat wave of the year), Early Summer extends from the final week of May through the end of June. During this season, the first cut of hay occurs throughout the lower Midwest. Strawberries, cherries and wild black raspberries ripen. Fireflies glow in the fields. These are the longest days of the year.

Deep Summer: This season contains three to five fronts and lasts from late June through the first week of August. Average temperatures are the highest of the year during most of the period; they start to fall on July 28th. Garden production peaks. Farmers harvest oats and winter wheat. Autumn bird migrations begin.

Late Summer: Late Summer contains four major fronts and extends from early August through the first weeks of September. Some Judas maples turn color as the Dog Days end. Blackberries ripen. Ragweed pollen drifts in the wind. Most wildflowers complete their cycle. Cricket and katydid song dominates the evenings.

Early Fall: This season has five to six significant cold fronts, and it lasts from early September to the middle of October. The danger of light frost now follows each front across the North. Major leafturn occurs on elms, cottonwoods, box elders, ashes and buckeyes, but most maples and oaks wait until Middle Fall. Farmers plant wheat and harvest their corn and soybeans.

Middle Fall: This period of the year contains five to six fronts and lasts from the middle of October through the first week or two of November. This is the period of peak maple and oak coloring, followed by the most intense leafdrop in the northern half of the country. Most farmers finish their harvest and the planting of winter grains. Bird migrations peak. Katydids and crickets fall silent.

Late Fall: The final season of the natural year contains five major high-pressure systems, lasts from early November through early December. The final leaves come down, the farm and garden cycle is completed and migrations end. The longest nights of the year begin throughout the United States.

THE MOONS FOR 2019

In the United States, the naming of moons has been associated with the early inhabitants of the continent, and newcomers learned some of those names from the peoples they encountered. Although different groups used different names for different moons, depending on their location (and the accompanying weather and sources of food), the following list is representative of what was used by some Native American nations:

January: Wolf Moon, February: Snow Moon,

March: Worm Moon April: Pink Moon, May: Flower Moon, June: Hot Moon or Strawberry Moon, July: Buck Moon, August: Sturgeon Moon September: Harvest Moon, October: Hunter's Moon, November: Beaver Moon, December: Cold Moon.

Even though some of these names are still in use today among people who read almanacks, I believe the tradition of naming is best continued by identifying lunar times within a more personal and local context.

To some, I suppose, that might mean the creation of names like the Super Bowl Moon or the World Series Moon. And such tags would certainly be more appropriate for sports fans than the Wolf Moon or Sturgeon Moon. Corporations might name moons for the different phases of the production and sales year. On a more intimate level, lovers might pick their moons from certain milestones in a relationship, the First Kiss Moon and so on.

My personal preference is to go to the local landscape to find some event in nature that coincides with the full Moon of a particular month. In the spring and summer months, the blooming of flowers and trees provides any number of suggestions. In fall and winter, other events such as leaf turn, leaf fall, migratory activity and indoor activities, like forcing bulbs or seeding of flowers and vegetables, offer ample variety for selection.

The most important thing about moons or any other natural phenomenon is that we notice them, and that we take them inside ourselves and allow them to bring some balance and harmony. Among all the changes of our lives, the changes of sky and of the seasons may be the least radical and disruptive. The stability of their rhythms can offset the instability of other parts of our lives. Naming can be a reminder to take part in that gift of compensation.

The following Moon names used in *Poor Will's Almanack for 2019* correspond to events related to seasonal change. The days listed are for the New Moon of each month. Of course, when one thing is happening, something else is happening, too. The narratives of each month provide numerous examples of what else is happening, too.

December 2018: **The Flowering Jessamine Moon**
January 5: **The Squashy Osage Moon**
February 4: **The Skunk Courting Moon**
March 6: **The Cabbage White Butterfly Moon**
April 5: **The Cows Switching Their Tails Moon**
May 4: **The Golden Buttercup Moon**
June 3: **The Milkweed Beetle Mating Moon**
July 2: **The Finches in theThistledown Moon**
July 31: **The Black Walnut Leafdrop Moon**
August 30: **The Autumn Apple Picking Moon**
September 28: **The High Leaf Color Moon**
October 27: **The Sleeping Frog Moon**
November 26: **The Silent Cricket Moon**
December 26: **The Pussy Willow Cracking Moon**

THE SUN'S POSITION IN THE ASTROLOGICAL ZODIAC

The Sun enters the following astrological signs on the following dates. The position of the Sun in the actual sidereal Zodiac is somewhat different, about one month later than passage into the astrological Zodiac sign.

***Poor Will's Almanack for 2019* uses the astrological markers, as they are more common in everyday parlance. The commentary on seasonal events when the Sun is in a particular sign takes this into consideration.**

December 22: (2018) Sagittarius into Capricorn
January 20: Capricorn into Aquarius
February 18: Aquarius into Pisces
March 20: Pisces into Aries
April 20: Aries into Taurus
May 21: Taurus into Gemini
June 21: Gemini into Cancer
July 23: Cancer into Leo
August 23: Leo into Virgo
September 23: Virgo into Libra
October 23: Libra into Scorpio
November 22: Scorpio into Sagittarius
December 22: Sagittarius into Capricorn

USING THE SEASONAL AFFECTIVE DISORDER (S.A.D.) STRESS INDEX

The S.A.D. Stress Index measures the natural phenomena which are assumed to be related to Seasonal Affective Disorder: the day's length, the percentage of probable sunlight, the weather and the phase of the moon.

In order to create the Index, each of those factors was given a value from zero to 25, and then the four values were combined onto a scale of one to 100. Interpretation is simple: the higher the number, the greater the stress.

Lunar phase and proximity to Earth produce the most dramatic swings in the Index. For example, full Moon days receive a rating of 25 and New Moon days receive a 20, whereas days on which the Moon enters its second and fourth quarters are given a lower rating, depending on the Moon's proximity to Earth (lunar perigee or apogee).

Ratings are based on tidal and sociological information that suggests the Moon is most influential when it is full, second-most influential when it is new and least influential at entry to its second and fourth phases.

Index readings are most useful in combination with a record of your own moods. Reference to the Index when you feel out of sorts may be a way of getting a feel for how Seasonal Affective Disorder influences your life.

In addition to the numbers that indicate the strength of particular forces that influence S.A.D., the seasonal descriptions in each month of the *Almanack* suggest events and objects in nature that can counter the negative effects of S.A.D. The following Guide to Activity of Creatures may also be used to evaluate periods of varying lunar influence.

PEAK ACTIVITY TIMES FOR CREATURES

This part of each monthly section of the *Almanack* is a guide to the effect of lunar position on living things.

Many people believe that livestock, humans, fish and game are more active when the Moon is overhead. The Moon is thought by many people to be less powerful, but still influential, when it is below your location, 12 hours before or after those times at which it is overhead.

In addition, peak lunar influence occurs at midday when the Moon is new, in the afternoon and evening when the Moon is in its first quarter, at night when the Moon is full and in its third quarter, and in the morning when the Moon is in its fourth quarter.

TRADITIONAL FARMING AND GARDENING LORE

In general, planting crops that bear their fruit above the ground is recommended when the Moon is waxing. Plant root crops, flower bulbs, trees and shrubs to promote root growth when the Moon is waning.

According to a number of studies, the Moon exerts less influence on ocean tides and on human and animal behavior when it comes into its second and fourth quarters. Therefore, it might make more sense to perform routine maintenance on your flock or herd near the date on which the Moon enters its second or fourth quarter.

On the other hand, tidal lunar influences have been shown to be greater at full Moon and New Moon times. You might expect more trouble with your animals, therefore, on or about New Moon and Full Moon.

Livestock care should be less difficult during the relatively stable times between frontal systems listed in each month's meteorology section.

THE CALENDAR OF FEAST DAYS

In this section, the *Almanack* lists the days on which farmers, gardeners and homesteaders might expect the public to have increased interest in their livestock or produce. This calendar is also useful when one is planning strategies for marketing to ethnic or religious groups.

INDEX OF ESSAYS BY BILL FELKER

The essays that appear on the first page of each month are taken from a nature column I have written for the *Yellow Springs News* since 1984.

January: *Solomon and Sheba in the Attic*
February: *South to the Edge of Winter*
March: *Lion Journal*
April: *Notes on Stability*
May: *Higher Time*
June: *Autobiography*
July: *Backyard Solar Eclipse*
August: *Cosmic Children*
September: *Reenactment*
October: *Virtues and Self-Sufficiency*
November: *Attachment and Befriending*
December: *Taking Stock*

A NOTE ON ALMANACK LITERATURE

Poor Will's readers have been contributing to my weekly and monthly columns since 1985. I include my favorite stories of recent years in each annual version of the *Almanack*.

Bill Felker

INDEX OF ALMANACK LITERATURE BY READERS OF *POOR WILL's ALMANACK*

Find these stories by going to the *last* pages of each month.

January: *Speaking with Mice* by Janet Stevens
    Our Black Pearl by Rachael Gwassa
February: *Wimpy, the Runt* by Eugenia Hermann
    Speaking with Flies by Janet Stevens
March: *Bruce and the Gelding* by Dawn Shovar
    The Squawk that Saved My New Winter Coat by Myrna Glass
April: *The Dog with the High IQ* by Ron Hocker
    Strutter Gets in Trouble by Ibbie Ledford
May: *The Escape Artist* by Richard Dietke
    Boss to the Rescue by Ann Witte
June: *A Timely Revelation* by Alonso Byrd
    Speaking with Mice II by Janet Stevens
July: *Pliny Fulkner's Amazing Fish Caller* by Mrs. Pliny Fulkner
    One of a Kind by Marlene Arcuri
August: *Smart Lamb* by Sonia Clements
    Tag in the Face by Ann Witte
September: *Did the Diet Make the Difference?* By Eugenia Hermann
    Bring the Hoe! by Sylvia P. Gibbons
October: *Granny in the Hole!* by Susan Perkins
    Singing Worms
November: *Beating the Devil* By Mrs. Fairy Huffine
    Crime and Punishment by J. W. Croninger
December: *A Sudden Snowstorm* by Rick Etter

All Things Bright and Beautiful by Sara Beck

The Time of Day
In *Poor Will's Almanack*

All times in this *Almanack* are given in Eastern Standard Time.

Capitalization of the Names of the Seasons

The names of the twelve sub-seasons of the year are capitalized in *Poor Will's Almanack:* Deep Winter, Late Winter, Early Spring, Middle Spring, Late Spring, Early Summer, Deep Summer, Late Summer, Early Fall, Middle Fall, Late Fall, Early Winter.

On the other hand, the four commonly used names for the longer traditional seasons (winter, spring, summer and fall) are not capitalized.

The words Sun, Moon, New Moon, Full Moon and Earth are capitalized in *Poor Will's Almanack.*

THE ALMANACK HOROSCOPE FOR CAPRICORN INTO AQUARIUS IN JANUARY 2019

After all, anybody is as their land and air is. Anybody is as the sky is low or high, the air heavy or clear and anybody is as there is wind or no wind there. It is that which makes them and the arts they make and the work they do and the way they eat and the way they drink and the way they learn and everything.

Gertrude Stein

The Gregorian Calendar

S	M	T	W	T	F	S
		1	2	3	4	5
6	7	8	9	10	11	12
13	14	15	16	17	18	19
20	21	22	23	24	25	26
27	28	29	30	31		

Solomon and Sheba in the Attic

My furnace is in the attic of my house, and that place is always warm in the coldest weather. During the later winter and Early Spring, I plant seeds under grow lights there.

Last year when I did my attic gardening, I found a stink bug crawling around on the table where I do my planting. I watched my stink bug and saw that he appeared harmless and very vulnerable. Once he fell off a leaf and lay on his back kicking until I picked him up and set him on his feet. I smelled my fingers then. No odor, really.

This year, I noticed another stink bug in the attic. I wondered if he had lived there by himself for the past twelve months. I looked around to see if there were more stink bugs. I found one more, but no more than that.

For some reason, it occurred to me that those two must be wise to survive isolated in the attic. So I named one Solomon (after the famous, wise king) and the other Sheba, after the Queen of Sheba, who was quite interested in that king. But I don't really know the anatomical gender of either bug. Who would care about the sex of two small creatures in the attic? Besides, I can't tell them apart.

While some people have told me they are overrun by stink bugs, I feel that my stink bugs are good company. My attic is low and cramped. No one has ever joined me planting seeds. I reflect that insects are under siege throughout the world these days, thanks to pesticides and global warming. I wonder if perhaps these two stink bugs are hiding with me from Armageddon.

And I wonder who besides Solomon and Sheba would be so unobtrusive, provide fellowship without destroying my solitude, require no food, no drink. Best of all, they do not fit the mold. They do not act like the fabled stink bugs of Orkin or

Terminex. They do not follow the entomological script. They follow their own counsel. They could be overrunning my house, but they are content to bask in the warmth of the grow lights and contemplate the luminescent April green of the sprouts. Solomon and Sheba have, it seems, found the Path. They might even be trying to show me their secret. I will see.

The Capricorn-Aquarius Sun

Perihelion, the point at which the Earth and the Sun are closest to one another, occurs on January 3 at 12:00 a.m. The Sun enters the Late Winter sign of Aquarius on January 20.

Having passed deep into Sagittarius and then to the far edge of Capricorn during December's Early Winter, the Sun slowly increases its declination in the sky, rising a little higher toward Aquarius throughout its brief residence in the day, lengthening shadows and sending messages to creatures large and small.

Solar influence brought sheep and goats to estrus as the Sun passed into the signs of Libra and Scorpio. Now Capricorn and Aquarius stimulate mating time for foxes and coyotes and nesting time for owls. Across the South, the Sun wakens hibernating black bears and opens the season of camellia bloom. Greenhouse orchids and jade trees blossom, too.

The Sunstop period during which the Sun's declination remains within less than a degree of winter solstice, comes to a close in middle Capricorn and by the first week of Aquarius, the night recedes a minute or two each day toward Early Spring.

Average temperatures start to rise throughout the nation under Aquarius. Sap runs in the maples. The day becomes more than an hour longer than it was at solstice.

When the Sun passes through Aquarius, then Late Winter arrives and the full onslaught of change starts to ride over the Northern Hemisphere, the momentum building, pulling the land back toward warmth and new life.

Cardinals, which sang only sporadically earlier in the month, begin consistent mating calls half an hour before dawn, doves often joining their song. The first major waves of robins and bluebirds cross the Ohio River. Squirrels chase each other through the trees. Along the highways, road kills attest to the increasing nighttime activities of skunks and opossums.

January 27 is a pivotal statistical date in the fortunes of winter. Throughout the country average temperatures, which had remained stable from the middle of January, climb one degree. That rise may not be obvious in any particular year, but it does represent the cumulative wisdom of all the years on record, revealing the inevitable turn of the Earth toward June.

Even unrecognized, these events and many more subtly transform the feel of the world and alter the sense of time and habitat. The horoscope, the January watching of time that includes the duration of the cold and darkness itself, nurtures anticipation and restlessness. The winter, often seeming unbearably long, feeds, even by its cruelty, hope and longing that spread the vague but exciting message: Something new is coming,

The Flowering Jessamine Moon and The Squashy Osage Fruit Moon

As the position of the Sun dictates the broader seasons and the major phases of Earth's weather, so the Moon accompanies and complements the solar directives, its tidal power influencing not only the great bodies of water but the rhythm of the movement of the atmosphere and the human psyche.

Even as most leafdrop and blooming ends

across the Northern states, the flowering of bright yellow Jessamine, in fencerows and lowlands throughout the states that border the Gulf of Mexico, marks the opening of Early Spring and opens the long encroachment of new life against the frozen wall of Deep Winter.

Across the range of the Osage orange, the softball-size fruit of that tree fell throughout the autumn and now turns brown and squashy during thaws that melt its protective covering of snow. The decay of these fruits, as well as the breakdown of last year's plant stalks, the scattering of seeds and berries, are all dials that tell the time of year and shape the emotional climate in which all creatures move.

January 5: The Flowering Jessamine Moon becomes the Squashy Osage Fruit Moon at 8:28 p.m.
The New Year's Eve of 2018, eventful as it was, did not fall under the spell of the New Moon, but now the weather of Deep Winter should definitely turn cruel.

January 8: The Moon reaches apogee at 11:29 a.m.
Lunar apogee (the Moon's position farthest from Earth) should soften the January 10 cold front, providing some relief from New Moon cold.

January 14: The Moon enters its second quarter at 1:46 a.m.
The Moon remains relatively weak today, allowing the low-pressure system that precedes the

Supermoon of January 21 to create a welcome but deceptive thaw.

January 21: The Moon is full at 12:16 a.m. Lunar perigee also occurs on this date, making this full Moon a full Supermoon.

A quickening of bird and small activity usually takes place when the Sun enters Aquarius (on January 20), and full Moon with perigee accentuates the change.

There will be a total lunar eclipse beginning at approximately 9:30 p.m. EST on January 21. The Moon will be completely eclipsed close to midnight.

January 27: The Moon enters its final quarter at 4:10 p.m.

As the Supermoon weakens, weather should moderate, and seasonal stress abate considerably.

The Planets

The significance of the planets and their influence on human affairs is an ancient concern with a language all its own.

While it is possible that the larger planets may influence Earth's weather and even the course of history, for time watchers, the larger and nearer planets can become complementary markers of the seasons, accompanying the Sun and stars to create a palate of beauty as well as to define the character and nuance of the night and its borders.

In Ophiuchus (between Libra and Scorpio), Jupiter and Venus are the Morning Stars this month, rising before dawn from the East. Venus is the brighter of the two. Saturn follows close behind in Sagittarius. Like any special display in the heavens, the appearance of giant Jupiter and Venus before Sunrise enhances the entry into the day.

Venus will appear close to the Moon on January 31 at 2:36 a.m. Jupiter will appear near the Moon at 2:37 a.m. on January 3, and on January 30 at 6:54 p.m.

Mars begins the year as an Evening Star in the southwest with Pisces.

The Stars

The star groups of the Summer Triangle (Cygnus, Aquila and Lyra) ride above the Sun in Capricorn throughout the day, chasing the autumn constellations into the west, forecasting the heat of July, coinciding with the January pollination seasons of pines, even in the coldest time of year.

At night, when Orion lies in the center of the southern sky, the Milky Way stretches from the northwest, through Perseus and down into the southeast. From the far eastern horizon, the spring planting star, Regulus, is rising, and in the northeast, the pointers of the Big Dipper are aligned east-west. In the west, October's Great Square is setting.

Divided in allegiance between Deep Summer and Deep Winter, the sky holds the Earth's inhabitants close to the fireside at night, but in the daytime all its constellations promise rebirth.

The Shooting Stars

January's shooting stars are the Quadrantids; they appear early in the first week of the month, most heavily on January 4, at the rate of about 35 per hour. Look for them before midnight in the eastern sky near Arcturus. The dark Moon will favor meteor watching, offering a benign context for the first of 2019's shooting stars.

S.A.D. Index in January

Capricorn and Aquarius in January bring the coldest weather, the cloudiest skies and the longest nights of the year to every state of the Union.

Full Moon and perigee on January 21 combine to produce intense lunar influence, making the third week of this month one of the most difficult periods of the year for those suffering from Seasonal Affective Disorder.

Key for Interpreting the S.A.D. Index:
Totals of 100 to 80: Severe stress
79 to 55: Severe to moderate stress
54 to 40: Moderate stress
39 to 25: Light to moderate stress

24 and below: Light stress

Day	Clouds	Weather	Day	Moon	Totals
January 1:	25	24	25	10	84
January 5:	25	25	24	20	94
January 14:	25	25	24	15	89
January 21:	25	25	24	30	104
January 31:	25	22	22	10	79

Peak Activity Times for Creatures

When the Moon is **above** the continental United States, creatures are typically most active. The second-most-active times occur when the Moon is **below** the Earth.

Activity is likely to increase at New Moon (January 5) and full Moon and at perigee (January 21), especially as the barometer falls in advance of cold fronts near those dates.

Date	Above	Below
January 1 – 4:	Mornings	Evenings
January 5 – 13:	Afternoon	Midnight to Dawn
January 14 – 20:	Evenings	Mornings
January 21 – 26:	Midnight to Dawn	Afternoons
January 27 – 31:	Mornings	Evenings

Meteorology
Based on Average Arrival of Weather Systems and the Phases of the Moon

*Unlike other commercial almanacks, **Poor Will's Almanack** integrates lunar conditions with the likely arrival times of weather systems, noting how the moon's phase and proximity to Earth could influence frontal behavior.*

High-pressure systems are due to cross the country on or around the following dates: January 1, 5, 10, 15, 19, 25, 31.

The first five January weather systems belong to the subseason of Deep Winter, the last two to Late Winter.

Readers in the East should add one to two days to specific days mentioned in the overviews, which are made from weather records in the Lower Midwest. In the Plains, subtract one to two days for best results.

Temperature ranges given in the weekly weather sections are based on averages in the lower Midwest. In order to estimate temperatures in their own regions, readers should subtract one degree for every 100 miles north of the 40th Parallel but add two degrees for every 100 miles south of the 40th Parallel.

If strong storms occur this month, weather patterns suggest that they will happen during the following periods: January 1-2, 8-12 and 19-24 (the transition time to Late Winter and the period of the Full Moon).

New Moon on January 5 and full Moon with lunar perigee (producing a Supermoon) on January 21 are likely to intensify the weather systems due around those dates.

Weekly Weather Estimates
Week 1

The warmest days of January's first quarter are typically the 3rd and the 6th, each having a 25 percent chance of highs above freezing. Cold comes too, however. The first major cold front of the year arrives the last day of December or the 1st or 2nd of January, and most days between the 1st and the 7th have a 30 to 40 percent chance of highs only in the 20s or teens. New Moon on January 5 this year increases the likelihood of cold.

Clouds usually dominate the sky this week: there is just a 40 percent chance of Sun between the 1st and 3rd, and there is even a 70 percent chance of completely overcast conditions on the 6th.

Precipitation is lightest on the 1st (a 30 percent chance), but heaviest on the 2nd and 3rd (around a 50 percent chance). Chances of precipitation on the other days this week are in the 40 percent range.

Week 2

Weather history for the second week of January shows rapidly increasing odds for colder weather. The 8th and 9th, which coincide with the arrival of the year's second major weather system, have the coldest records of all, each with a 50 to 55 percent chance of highs below 30. Below-zero readings occur most often on the 9th, 11th, and 16th (20 percent of the years in my record).

With a general increase in the cold, skies have fewer clouds this week of the year, and the 12th, 13th, 15th and 16th bring a 60 percent chance of Sun. The cloudiest day of the week is usually the 14th. Precipitation occurs two years out of three between the 12th and the 14th.

Week 3

After the 15th, statistics show a warming trend that brings a 35 percent chance of a high above freezing. The possibility of mild weather is enhanced by the approach of the fourth cold front of the month. The low-pressure trough leading that front often brings in warm southerly winds. During January's third week in 1890, the longest record-breaking thaw in Lower Midwestern history warmed temperatures into the upper 60s for three days. That is not likely in 2019, since the Squashy Osage Moon will bring frigid conditions when it becomes full on the 21st.

Days when the temperature does not rise above zero occur more often this week than in any other week, and morning lows below zero occur more in the third week of January than in any other week of the year. The driest day of the period is the 18th, with just a 25 percent chance of showers or flurries. All the rest of the days carry about a 50 percent chance of rain or snow.

Week 4

After full Moon, the likelihood of cooler conditions continues, making January 25 and 26 two of the crueler days of the month. But although the 31st can bring subfreezing temperatures almost half the time, that day introduces a possibility for highs well above freezing. Between the 26th and 28th, dry conditions prevail 75 percent of the years, and the 27th is often the sunniest day in January. The 30th is the cloudiest day.

Best Lunar Planting Times

Seed bedding plants near the New Moon (January 5). Plant the spring garden throughout the South, root crops under the dark last quarter of the Golden Jessamine Moon, crops that produce their fruit above the ground in the first quarter of the Squashy Osage Moon.

Calendar of Feast Days and Holidays for Farmers, Gardeners and Homesteaders

The calendar year offers a complement to the year in nature, frequently connecting social traditions to phases of the Moon and pivotal times for agricultural activities. In general, both societal and climatic markers influence attitudes and behavior in humans, inviting the time watcher to ruminate about and take advantage of the various tones of the year's passage.

January 5, 2019: The pre-Lenten carnival season begins near this date, one month before Mardi Gras. Explore the market for lambs and kids for cookouts throughout the South during this period. Even at the month's darkest period and even for those for whom Easter has no spiritual meaning, this season sets the stage for the end of the cruelest time.

January 7, 2019: Plough Monday A traditional day, dating from the Middle Ages for the beginning of the farm and garden year.

January 6, 2019: Epiphany (Three-Kings Day) Many Christians celebrate this feast with a fine meal and religious services. Milk-fed lambs are often in demand for this market. The feast can also be celebrated on the Sunday between January 2 and January 8.

Almanack Literature
Speaking With Mice
by Janet Stevens

My cabin is back in the woods on a country road. Since I am there only occasionally, the wild things look on it as part of their range. One spring when I opened up, I picked up my wide-spouted aluminum teakettle, and a mouse darted from the spout. I tipped the lid, finding a nest of wee ones, their heads looking like the pink erasers on pencils. The family was my guest until the babies could travel.

After I cleaned the cabin, I sat down for a breather. "Mice," I said, "I don't much relish this cleanup business."

Beady eyes were on me, pink ears were listening, little minds were reaching out. I thought-spoke: "You are dear little beasties, and I value your place in the scheme of things. I just wish you didn't track up the place so. I don't begrudge you the food you eat, nor a nest in the woodbox, but can't you leave my stuff alone?"

Laying a paper on the table, I set out a cut apple and a scatter of popcorn, and did the same at a spot near the door. Mice and I didn't really bargain, for we understood one another. I saw their needs: food, and shelter from foxes and owls. They saw mine: a habitable retreat for rest and study. In this world and in this space, there is a place for each of us. After I thought-talked with them explaining this, I closed the cabin and went home.

Word has gotten round. My things have not been soiled, chewed nor disturbed for years now. Well, they did eat some soap, preferring the homemade to the commercial. Chipmunks had once started to dig around the foundation, but that stopped. There's a woodchuck settlement within thirty feet of the cabin, but it has not undermined the foundation.

I feel very safe there, for the wildlings and I are never adversaries, as we cooperate in the space granted to us.

Our Black Pearl
By Rachael Gwassa

Our flock of maiden ewes was due to start lambing in a couple of days. We were working on fencing a new pasture for them, and it was nearly finished. They were currently sharing a pasture with our small herd of pastured pork.

I went out as soon as I woke in the morning (yet in my pajamas!) and flashed the spotlight around the pasture. Then I saw the hogs in a huddle, a forlorn ewe and then I heard the bleat of a lamb!

I screamed to my husband, "There's a lamb out

there, and the hogs are getting it! Hurry!" He shouted at them to distract the hogs while I ran to turn off the electric fence. I ran in and grabbed the lamb, alive but not looking very lively. It was a lovely black ewe lamb with the end of her tail eaten off, and her umbilical cord pulled out a couple of inches. Other than that she appeared all right.

She could not stand. I tubed colostrum into her immediately. We took her to the vet later that day, but he said there was nothing he could do for her; we should clean the umbilical area a couple of times a day. And so we did.

She would not suck a bottle. I tubed her milk five times a day. She could not walk. Bowel movements were painful for her; she moaned at each one. On the fourth day I thought she would die: she was lying flat out on her side, not moving. That day I didn't feed her.

Incredibly, the next day she looked better. I believe the fasting day actually improved her condition. It allowed her digestive system time to rest and heal. And so I tubed her milk again. On the sixth day, she got up and walked around a little. On the seventh day, she actually started drinking from a bottle!

We bottle-fed her for the next five weeks. We couldn't put her in with the other lambs, because they would suck on the protruding umbilical cord.

She became our pet, and the farm dog was her companion. They would take naps together on the porch of our farm store, much to the delight of our customers!

She is completely healed now, living with the rest of the flock and awaiting the birth of her first lamb. When the farm dog comes into the pasture with me, she comes to greet him happily.

We named her Pearl, because we saved her from the swine. (*Cast not your pearls before the swine, for they will surely trample them asunder.* Matthew 7, 6)

Bill Felker

THE ALMANACK HOROSCOPE FOR AQUARIUS INTO PISCES IN FEBRUARY 2019

Different atmospheric conditions – different kinds of weather are, precisely different moods. Wind, rain, snow, fog, hail, open skies, heavy overcast – each…affects the relation between our body and the living land in a specific way, altering the tenor of our reflections and the tonality of our dreams.

David Abram

The Gregorian Calendar

S	M	T	W	T	F	S
					1	2
3	4	5	6	7	8	9
10	11	12	13	14	15	16
17	18	19	20	21	22	23
24	25	26	27	28		

South to the Edge of Winter

From the deep cold of the Ohio Valley, we drove south to find the last days of winter and the first of spring.

The snow cover disappeared after we passed through the mountains into Virginia. There the rolling land appeared pale and soft like the coat of a sleeping winter beast.

Charlotte, North Carolina, to Savannah and Tybee Island, Georgia: Full Sun and cold (frost on the windshield), patches of light snow and frozen swamp between Columbia, South Carolina, and the coast, black ice on the streets of Savannah, snow holding to the dunes, temperature near 40 degrees.

The bitter weather of January's first week throughout so much of the Southeast and the near complete kill of flowers from South Carolina to the Gulf made it easier to discover a relatively narrow space in which winter had stalled and in which the normal January flora of the peninsula could hold its own.

A little below Jacksonville, Florida, the first signs of a more gentle season: some clover and chickweed foliage. The roadside grass became taller and greener as we went along, and when we reached Merritt Island, about halfway down the peninsula, we found that frost had caused only a little damage there, and numerous plants were in bloom: several violet azalea bushes in full flower; many violet and magenta bougainvilleas; Spanish needles (*Bidens pilosa*), the most common wildflower of the area this time of year; a sprawling, large-flowered climbing aster mostly gone to seed, perhaps the very last flower of the old year.

Having found or pretended to find the lacuna between seasons, I walked the beach, the rhythm of the ocean like the daybook journal of home itself, pulling me back and forth from one year to another in a sequence of memories and associations, waves rising and falling like days, place knitting time into fabric of water and sand.

David Abram suggests that different atmospheric conditions create "precisely different moods," and that they "alter the tenor of our reflections and the tonality of our dreams." My personal natural history, my history in nature and my trip from the Ohio River to the sea were cues for fantasy. All of the material world and its transformations and its connections were mnemonic phenomena, evocative forms, flimsy and web-like, fog-like mists of images and feelings that created a true phenology of parallels within which not only did the part represent the whole, but also the signs, conjuring emotion and knowledge, became what they signified.

The Aquarius-Pisces Sun

Just after the Groundhog Day Thaw is over (typically by February 4), the Sun rushes toward Early Summer, climbs past a declination of 16 degrees, reaches about 40 percent of the way to equinox by February 12, and on the 18th, Cross-Quarter Day, the Sun reaches its halfway point to equinox, entering the Early Spring sign of Pisces at the same time. And on February 24, the Sun reaches a declination of over nine and a half degrees, 60 percent of the way to solstice.

As the Sun moves from the sign of Aquarius (early and middle February) to Pisces (late February), precedents create promise and potential for the fledgling season. Almost every year, skunk mating season begins by the end of the Groundhog Day Thaw. Salamander breeding time opens in the first mild rains, and bobbing blue jays announce blue jay courting season. Doves called occasionally throughout December and January; now their full mating time swells and extends the predawn songs of cardinals and titmice.

Along the Gulf of Mexico, the Aquarius-Pisces Sun creates the seasons of violets, wintersweet, Lenten roses, strawberry and jasmine blooming seasons. In northern Mexico, monarch butterflies fly together toward the Texas border. They will arrive in the United States during March, and their offspring will find the Midwest in Deep Summer.

Firefly season starts in southern Florida. In the lower Midwest, turkeys come together for turkey flocking season and deer move into herds. In Arkansas, rhubarb leafing coincides with henbit leafing in Lexington, Kentucky.

The Squashy Osage Fruit Moon
and
The Skunk Courting Moon

The ebbing and flowing of the Moon under the influence of the Aquarius-Pisces Sun, helps to create dramatic shifts in weather as well as to stimulate changes in flora and fauna. The volatility of the Skunk Courting Moon accentuates solar influence, and the mix of warming and freezing, Sun and clouds, encourages skunks (and other small mammals) to wander the night in search of mates. Under this Moon, pussy willows emerge all the way, maple sap runs into buckets and the early bulbs – snowdrops, aconites and snow crocus – send up foliage in northern states and come into full bloom across the South.

February 4: The Skunk Courting Moon is new at 4:04 p.m.
The coincidence of New Moon with the average time for an end to the Groundhog Day Thaw suggests that today and the following week will be much colder than average.

February 5: The Moon reaches apogee (its position farthest from Earth) at 4:26 a.m.
Lunar apogee may soften the cold as the Moon moves toward entry into its mild second quarter.

February 12: The Moon enters its second quarter at 5:26 p.m.
Lunar phase and position will help to make the middle of February a time of major thaw – and of skunk courting!

February 19: The Moon reaches perigee (its position closest to Earth) at 4:06 a.m., and the Moon is full at 10:54 a.m. Perigee and full Moon make a Supermoon, the second of 2019.
The Moon will definitely end the middle-February thaw, bringing a "Snowdrop Winter" to the South and along the 40th Parallel.

February 25: The Moon enters its final quarter at 6:28 a.m.
Weak lunar position augers well for relatively mild conditions as February ends. The first March days should be "lamb-like."

The Planets

♃ ♄ ♂ ♀

If the planets and their position have significance to those who pay attention to traditional astrology, a time watcher (horoscoper) might find in the observation of the planets a comforting corollary to watching the Sun and the stars and their reflection in the maturing of the landscape. A follower of the Morning Star is rarely disconnected from nature or from her or himself.

This month, Jupiter remains the earliest Morning Star, rising a few hours past midnight in Ophiuchus. Moving retrograde from Ophiuchus and its tryst with Jupiter into Sagittarius, Venus arrives on the horizon just before dawn, with Saturn, low in the east, following well behind.

Red Mars moves retrograde from Pisces to Aries, visible in the west after dark.

The Stars

By ten o'clock in the evening in the first week in February, giant Orion begins to move west from its dominating January position in the center of the southern sky. The star grouping of Canis Major takes its place along the horizon, with Sirius, the Dog Star, the brightest light in the whole night sky. Sirius, along with Procyon (the large star to the upper left of Sirius) and Betelgeuse (the reddish left shoulder of Orion) form what appears from our position on Earth to be an equilateral triangle.

The Great Square sets in the west before midnight during February's second week. Perseus follows Cassiopeia into the northwest. Spring's Regulus will be well up in the sky on the other side of the horizon in the constellation Leo. Early

Summer's planting guide, Arcturus, is visible just before midnight in the northeast on February 12th.

By the third week in February, Procyon, the largest star of Canis Minor, replaces the Dog Star due south near 10:00 p.m. Above it, find the twins of Gemini, Castor and Pollux. To the right, Orion and the Milky Way have shifted deep into the west, a simple sign that Early Spring has begun. If you are looking for the North Star, the Big Dipper has moved well into the northeastern sky, up from its low December and January position, and its pointers, the outside stars of the dipper, are easily found. On the 17th, the first stars of Deep Summer's Hercules appear in the northeast after 10:00 p.m.

In the last week of February, the early night sky tells of Early Spring. Looking east, you can almost forget that cold Orion fills the west. Just a little to the right and down from the Big Dipper, May's Regulus is shining in the constellation Leo. The faint stars of lanky Hydra spread along the horizon. Due east, the most prominent star is Arcturus, which will be overhead this time of night when the first fireflies appear.

S.A.D. Stress Index

The likelihood of seasonal stress begins to fall steadily throughout February. Even though clouds usually continue to deprive the human brain of the benefits of sunlight, the length of the day complements the slowly improving temperatures, and the S.A.D. Index dips more frequently into 70s when the Moon lies in its weaker phases.

On the other hand, the second Supermoon of 2019 occurs on February 19, increasing the likelihood of severe weather and seasonal stress. Since the night has shortened considerably since January's Supermoon, however, the likelihood of seasonal stress should be much less than during full Moon time last month.

In addition, the harsh February elements tracked by the Index can be countered by paying attention to the Morning Stars and the phases of the Moon, and the radical events in nature that follow the Sun's entry into the sign of Pisces.

Key for Interpreting the S.A.D. Index:
Totals of 100 to 80: Severe stress
79 to 55: Severe to moderate stress
54 to 40: Moderate stress
39 to 25: Light to moderate stress
24 and below: Light stress

Day	Clouds	Weather	Day	Moon	Total
February 4:	23	24	20	20	87
February 12:	22	20	18	15	75
February 19:	22	19	18	30	89
February 27:	22	18	17	15	72

Peak Activity Times for Creatures

The following traditional guide to lunar position shows when the Moon is above or below the country, and, therefore, the portion of the day or night during which livestock, people, fish and game are typically the most active and the hungriest.

Activity is likely to increase at New Moon (February 4) and full Moon at perigee (February 19), especially as the barometer falls in advance of cold fronts near those dates.

Ordinarily, the Moon is most powerful when it is overhead (above your position).

Date	Above	Below
February 1 – 3:	Mornings	Evenings
February 4 – 11:	Afternoons	Midnight to Dawn
February 12 – 18:	Evenings	Mornings
February 19 – 24:	Midnight to Dawn	Afternoons
February 25 – 28:	Mornings	Evenings

Meteorology
Based on Average Arrival of Weather Systems and the Phases of the Moon

Significant cold waves are due to cross the United States around the following dates: February 3, 6, 11, 15, 20, 24 and 27. The first four February weather systems belong to the subseason of Late Winter, the last three to Early Spring.

Readers in the East should add one to two

days to specific days mentioned in the overviews. In the Plains, subtract one to two days for best results. Temperature ranges given in the weekly weather sections are based on averages in the lower Midwest. In order to estimate approximate temperatures in their own regions, readers should subtract one degree for every 100 miles north of the 40th parallel but add two degrees for every 100 miles south of the 40th Parallel.

If strong storms occur this month, they will be most likely to strike on or around February 2-4, 6-9, 14-18 and 24-27. **New Moon on February 4 and full Moon, combined with lunar perigee, on February 19 are likely to increase the intensity of the weather systems that typically arrive near those dates.**

Weekly Weather Estimates
Week 1

The first two days of February often bring a Groundhog Day Thaw and mild temperatures in the 50s and 60s to the Lower Midwest, the Middle Atlantic Region and the East. Beginning on the 3rd, however, conditions typically become chillier: the likelihood of below-zero temperatures becomes the greatest of the entire winter, and the chances of highs just in the 30s or below remains steady at 60 percent. New Moon on February 4 this year should make a frigid end to the Groundhog Day Thaw. The second barometric high of the month arrives near the 6th and generally redoubles the cold.

The driest days of February's first quarter are often the 7th and 8th, each bringing just a 25 percent chance of rain or snow. The wettest are the

1st (with a 55 percent chance of precipitation), and the 3rd and 6th (each with a 40 percent chance). The sunniest day, with almost a 70 percent chance of at least partly cloudy skies, is the 4th.

Week 2

The second quarter of February is typically very cold, with high temperatures in the 30s or below occurring better than 70 percent of the time. The likelihood of below-zero temperatures falls to half of that of last week, however. The 11th ushers in the third major cold wave of the month, and this is typically the last severe front of winter for Southern states.

By the 14th, chances of highs in the 20s or below fall to only 20 percent along the 40th Parallel, and by the 15th, chances of spring warmth above 50 degrees jump to 40 percent, the highest so far this year. This change is so dramatic on regional weather charts, that February 14 can easily be called the beginning of Early Spring, a six week period of changeable conditions during which milder weather gradually overwhelms the cold.

Precipitation is generally light between the 7th and the 10th. Between the 11th and the 15th, however, each day carries about a 50 percent chance of rain or snow.

Week 3

The third quarter in February is statistically one of the most exciting of the entire year at average elevations along the 40th Parallel. Chances of highs in the 20s or below remain low at 20 percent during the first part of the week, and then, for the first time since late November, fall to 10 percent by the end of the week. Chances of highs in the 40s or above climb to 70 percent by the 20th, and then between the 18th and the 23rd, chances of highs in the 50s or 60s reaches an average of 35 percent per day, the first time that has happened since December 10.

And in one of the most radical weather changes of the year, the weekly chances of an afternoon in the 50s or 60s swell from last week's one in ten to five in ten. Although below-zero temperatures can occur at this time of the year, February's third quarter is the second-last period in which such cold might be expected (March's first week is the very last).

On the other hand, even though the fifth high-pressure system of the month, which passes through around the 20th, is typically a mild one, this February's Supermoon on the 19th will almost surely put an end to the Early Spring warm-up. There is a 30 percent chance of precipitation on most days this week. The 20th is the day least likely to be wet, bringing just a 20 percent chance of rain or snow. The likelihood of clouds is high: 60 percent of the days offer no sunshine at all. The average amount of snowfall for this week, however, is ordinarily the lowest of the month.

Week 4

The fourth week of February is usually Snowdrop Winter Week along the 40th Parallel, a time of meteorological ambivalence, promising spring then backsliding. Still influenced by the

Supermoon of the 19th, this week is likely to be the windiest of the month, and colder temperatures often remain until the approach of March. While 50s and 60s each come 5 percent of the time, and 40s are recorded 30 percent of the years, highs only in the 20s or 30s occur the remaining 50 percent, and chances of a high in the teens are not infrequent. Snow falls 35 percent of the years on the 24th, and five years in ten on the 25th. But the 25th is also the last day in Early Spring that chances of snow get so high.

Best Lunar Planting Times

Seed bedding plants near the New Moon (February 4). Plant the spring garden throughout the South, root crops under the dark last quarter of the Squashy Osage Moon, crops that produce their fruit above the ground in the first quarter of the Skunk Courting Moon. Perform animal maintenance as the Moon is waning, after February 20.

A Calendar of Feast Days and Holidays for Farmers, Gardeners and Homesteaders

February 5, 2019: Tet, Vietnamese New Year and Chinese New Year The Chinese market is often strong throughout the winter, favoring sheep and goats in the 60 to 80-pound live-weight range.

February 27, 2019: Dominican Republic Independence Day Areas that have a sizeable population of residents from the Dominican Republic may show an increase in sales of lambs and kids that weigh between 20 to 35 pounds.

Almanack Literature
Wimpy, the Runt
By Eugenia Hermann

My father was a butcher at an Ohio packing plant during World War II. Frequently, he would bring a "runt" pig home for my mother to feed out, either for our own consumption or for resale.

One runt that arrived was a pint-sized piglet named Wimpy. He was really small and young. At the same time, our Springer Spaniel dog had puppies, and before anyone realized it, she had adopted the pig to nurse alongside her puppies.

Wimpy was totally happy with his adoption and grew quickly. He became very attached to the dog, following her everywhere, including going on hunting jaunts with her. More than once, the neighbors called my mother to tell her that Wimpy was caught in a fence somewhere. Mom would have to go rescue him and bring him home.

Weaning Wimpy became a major problem, however. He was the size of the dog and still wanted to nurse. Mom would keep the dog in the house and try to keep Wimpy in the barn, but to no avail. The climax occurred when Wimpy tore down the screen door trying to find his "mommy."

Regretfully, Wimpy was one young piggy who had to go to market early.

Speaking With Flies
By Janet Stevens

One summer Sunday after church, we decided to have dinner at a small restaurant nearby. We took a table, as the kitchen behind the counter made it too warm to sit at the counter.

A few flies hung over the ketchup and the sugar bowl, making nuisances of themselves. Tim was about to ask for a fly swatter, when Eldon said, "Come on, Janet, send these pesky flies away. You can do it. I've seen you work with flies and wasps at your cabin."

I looked at the flies, and explained to them that they were interfering with our pleasure at our meal. What's more, they were in danger of getting swatted if they persisted in hanging around. All this was done in a little quiet inner space I created for the flies and me. Then I said: "If you'll go over by the window, I'll see that no one bothers you."

Most courteously, they flew to the window. This raised a laugh. Then, with a smirk, I said proudly, "See, they obey me, and know I'm their boss."

The flies got the gist of what I had said, too, turned, and flew back to the table. That bratty being sitting there was not going to take credit for what they had so graciously done.

The laughter rose even higher.

Bill Felker

THE ALMANACK HOROSCOPE FOR PISCES INTO ARIES IN MARCH 2019

Without observation of events and objects, there is no visible time or space. The creation of any seasonal or geographic fabric is a matter of filling the emptiness of unawareness with detail. Actually, the details are not peripheral but central. They are the only things. This is common sense: Any named unit of space or time is only the sum of its parts: What you see and smell and hear and taste and touch is what you get.

A Daybook for the Year In Yellow Springs

The Gregorian Calendar

S	M	T	W	T	F	S
					1	2
3	4	5	6	7	8	9
10	11	12	13	14	15	16
17	18	19	20	21	22	23
24	25	26	27	28	29	30
31						

Lion Journal

March had come in like a lion. And in the morning, I walked through town along the road to the songs of sparrows and calls of crows, southeast into woods of Osage and scrub black walnuts and box elders.

All the branches were coated with ice, were shining in the Sun, the world bright, steaming from the melting water.

I moved out of the open road and the noise of the city into a protective hive of reflected light and a bee-like murmuring that grew stronger as I entered the woods and that took away all my attention from the world outside.

I was at peace. I walked slowly stroking the bark of trees slippery from the storm. The ice dropped around me, pieces like brittle cocoons or cicada ectoskeletons, fossils of the branches, the winter's hulls, crisp calices of raindrops shattered in the March Sun.

I felt as if I were walking in rain and hail, but the sky was so pure blue. There was no wind at all, but the air was bitter cold, and so it seemed to me that it was the warmth of the Sun alone that undid the branches and created the clatter or a ticking and then a hum and song of Early Spring, distracting me from the possibility there could be other sounds from the highway nearby or from the sparrows and crows I had always heard here.

The new day collapsed all around me, into my hair, down the back of my coat, onto my wrists above my gloves. I broke off an icicle, licked it and then bit down on its tip, spring melting in my mouth. I stepped deliberately into layers of the bangles of the storm, crunching and crackling my way into the open field, where suddenly the grass was soft and silent, and I could hear birds again and cars passing on the road half a mile away.

The Pisces-Aries Sun

Daylight Saving Time begins at 2:00 a.m. on Sunday, March 10.

Equinox occurs at 4:58 p.m. March 20. The Sun enters the Middle Spring sign of Aries on March 21. When one thing happens, then something else is happening too. That is the most basic rule of phenology. And as the Sun travels through Pisces toward Aries, the day's length triggers the start of the robin mating chorus in the early morning dark.

When the robin chorus begins before sunrise, then pollen forms on pussy willow catkins, and the first mosquito bites, and the foliage of yarrow, mallow, phlox, columbine, coneflower, goldenrod, buttercup, New England aster and Queen Anne's lace is coming up.

Robins have found their way to every yard, knowing that worms will be waiting for them, at the same time that the tufted titmouse courts in spirals, when flickers and purple martins migrate and willow trees glow yellow green, pacing the new privet leaves, black raspberry, multiflora rose, clematis and coralberry leaves.

Lilac and mock orange buds glow defiantly against the gray sky. Skunk cabbage is red and fat in the swamp flats. Chickweed and dandelions flower in the woods. Earliest henbit blossoms in the gardens.

When Pisces and Aries rule the Sun and robins sing before dawn, the first blue lungwort flowers open and bleeding hearts get bushy. The first tulip bud has formed. The early honeysuckle bushes green the countryside, and the tree line is tinged with red from flowering maples.

Snow-on-the-mountain in the garden is pacing the waterleaf in the wetlands to the mating songs of red-winged blackbirds in the swamps and the gobbling of turkeys in the deep woods and ducks arriving at lakes and rivers in their mating plumage.

And if you see or hear just one of these events, one piece of the Sun's passage from the sign of Pisces into Aries, you know that all these other things, and so many more, are happening around you.

Phases of Skunk Courting Moon and the Cabbage White Butterfly Moon

White cabbage butterflies are the surest sign of the full sweep of Early Spring, and the Cabbage White Butterfly Moon warms them from the chrysalis stage early in Pisces throughout the South, early in Aries throughout the Northern states. Once you notice the familiar white cabbage butterfly, then you know the more elusive mourning cloak butterflies and the question mark butterflies and the tortoise shell butterflies and the tiny blues are flying too.

When you see cabbage butterflies, then you know that gold finches are turning gold, and you may soon see ants working on the sidewalk. If you see a cabbage butterfly, then you know that catfish have begun spring feeding and breeding. If you see a cabbage butterfly, then green bottle flies have hatched and termites are swarming, looking for new, sweet wood to eat.

When cabbage butterflies are out, then soft sprouts of touch-me-nots have emerged in the wetlands and the branches of weeping willow trees are turning pale yellow-green as their buds expand. In the city, *cornus mas* shrubs produce golden blossoms, promising forsythia in the first week of Middle Spring.

If you see a white cabbage butterfly on your way to work, you can know that Middle Spring's hepatica and twinleaf are pushing out in the sanctuary of the woodlands. Toad trillium and Dutchman's britches are ready to open there, the entire spectrum of wildflowers surging to encounter April.

Under the White Cabbage Butterfly Moon, white tundra swans reach Lake Erie and wolf spiders hatch in the gray fields. Starlings and crows continue to pair off and select nesting sites.

Coltsfoot opens in the full of the White Cabbage Butterfly Moon throughout the mountains of Pennsylvania and West Virginia. Cherry trees blossom in the nation's capital. Azaleas and camellias bloom in the Deep South. In the Ohio Valley, the first bluebells press through the mulch, no matter what the weather. Snowdrops, aconites and snow crocuses reach the peak of their seasons.

March 4: The Skunk Courting Moon reaches apogee (its position farthest from Earth) at 7:25 a.m. *Lunar phase and position augur well for a relatively mild beginning of March, conducive to the month coming in like a lamb.*

March 6: The Cabbage White Butterfly Moon is new at 11:04 a.m.
New Moon is likely to prevent March from arriving like a lamb) and bring increased chances of precipitation in advance of the March 5 cold front.

March 14: The Moon enters its second quarter at 5:27 a.m.
Lunar position favors a relatively gentle middle March.

March 19: The Moon is at perigee (its position closest to Earth) at 2:47 p.m.
But today's lunar perigee should chill the advance of Early Spring with wind and snow.

March 20: The Moon is full at 8:43 p.m.
Don't expect mild weather with the arrival of equinox. The full Moon with perigee (a "near" Supermoon) pretty much guarantees cruel conditions.

March 27: The Moon enters its final quarter at 11:10 p.m.
March came in like a lamb and will go out like a lamb, thanks to the waning crescent Moon moving away from Earth toward apogee.

March 29: The Moon reaches apogee at 7:14 p.m.

The Planets

♃ ♄ ♂ ♀

Accompanying those who choose to travel through the signs of Pisces-Aries sky time with more than Moon, three of the major planets appear before dawn this month, creating a sequence that starts just after midnight.

Jupiter begins the procession of Morning Stars, coming up with Ophiuchus and rising higher in the eastern sky as the night goes on. Following Jupiter along the southern horizon, Saturn travels with Sagittarius as robins start their mating calls, and Venus follows Saturn in Capricorn, replacing Jupiter as the brightest Morning Star in the east before dawn.

Rising later than these three planets, Mars follows Aries, almost obscured by the brilliance of the day but following the Sun, to arrive above the western horizon in time to become the Evening Star.

The Stars

The stellar horoscope of the year's third month tracks the departure of the coldest time of year, offering starwatchers, in even the northernmost states, clear signs of change.

By the first week of March (the second week of the Sun in Pisces) Orion has moved off to the west by midnight and Corvus, May's corn and soybean planting constellation, appears on the horizon. Spica, which will be centered in the southern sky as peak planting ends this Late Spring, emerges from the east. June's Corona Borealis follows it.

As the Sun rises higher in the sky, more Early Spring stars take over the night sky. The fertile planting constellation of Cancer is almost overhead between Pollux and Regulus. Hydra follows at its heels. May's Virgo approaches along the southeast horizon. The Big Dipper swings deeper into the southern sky.

Under the sign of Aries, all of winter's stars cluster together in the far west just a few hours after dark. They take the Milky Way with them and completely disappear from view by three o'clock in the morning.

The S.A.D. Stress Index

Cloud cover and inclement weather continue to hold Index readings relatively high during March. The day keeps lengthening, however, and improved meteorological conditions toward the end of the month push the Index numbers down into the middle 50s and 60s after equinox.

As in previous months, lunar phase and proximity to Earth increase the likelihood that you may experience S.A.D. The period near equinox is expected to be especially troublesome, since perigee, the full White Cabbage Butterfly Moon and the traditional March 20 weather system converge at that time.

However, antidotes for stress caused by weather, the day's length, clouds and lunar positions, are numerous. Those who watch the landscape, listen for birds and follow the stars may encounter an entirely different context for their moods, one that dissipates winter gloom and gives March the power of prophesy.

Key for Interpreting the S.A.D. Index:
Totals of 100 to 80: Severe stress
79 to 55: Severe to moderate stress
54 to 40: Moderate stress
39 to 25: Light to moderate stress
24 and below: Light stress

Day	Clouds	Weather	Daylight	Moon	Totals
March 6:	21	18	17	16	72
March 14:	20	16	15	8	59
March 20:	18	13	14	30	75
March 27:	17	12	12	15	56

Peak Activity Times for Creatures

The following traditional guide to lunar position shows when the Moon is above or below the country, and, therefore, the portion of the day or night during which livestock, people, fish and game are typically the most active and the hungriest.

Activity is likely to increase at New Moon (March 6) and perigee (March 19) and full Moon (March 20), especially as the barometer falls in advance of cold fronts near those dates.

Ordinarily, the Moon is most powerful when it is overhead (above your position).

Date	Above	Below
March 1 – 5:	Mornings	Evenings
March 6 – 13:	Afternoons	Midnight to Dawn
March 14 – 19:	Evenings	Mornings
March 20 – 27:	Midnight to Dawn	Afternoons
March 28 – 31:	Mornings	Evenings

Meteorology
Based on Average Arrival of Weather Systems and the Phases of the Moon

Major March weather systems usually cross the Mississippi River on March 2, 5 (usually the most severe front of the month), 9 (ordinarily followed by quite mild temperatures), 14, 19 (frequently the second-coldest front of March), 24 (often followed by the best weather so far in the year) and 29.

Readers in the East should add one to two days to specific days mentioned in the overviews. In the Plains, subtract one to two days for best results. Temperature ranges given in the weekly weather sections are based on averages in the lower Midwest. In order to estimate temperatures in their own regions, readers should subtract one degree for every 100 miles north of the 40th parallel but add two degrees for every 100 miles south of the 40th Parallel.

Major storms are most likely to occur on the days between March 9 and 14, and between March 19 and 30. **New Moon on March 6 and full Moon on the 20th (combined with perigee on the 19th) are likely to bring frost deep into Southern gardens and increased chances of storms across the North. Apogee on March 4 should soften the effect of the New Moon on the 6th.**

Weekly Weather Estimates
Week 1

Although the first cold front of March arrives on the 3rd, bringing a 60 percent chance of highs in the 40s or below, the first quarter of the month also brings a steady 5-10 percent chance of an afternoon in the 70s for the first time since early November. In fact, 70s occur more often on the 2nd and 3rd at average elevations along the 40th Parallel than on any days in the first three weeks of March. And 50s or 60s occur about 30 percent of the time through the week, similar to what happened during February's third week. This time, however, the percentage seldom drops below that level until Late Fall. Also this week, the percentage of afternoon highs in the teens and 20s drops to between 10 and 15 percent per day, the first time that has happened since early December.

The skies continue to brighten, with the 3rd bringing a 70 percent chance of Sun, and the 7th an 80 percent chance. The wettest days of the week are the 4th, 5th and 6th. New Moon on March 6 is likely to bring deep cold to the end of the week on the back of the March 5 cold front, increasing the chances of precipitation before the arrival of that front.

Week 2

March's second quarter brings one more major pivot in the year's weather patterns. The rate of Early Spring's advance quickens, and odds for milder weather increase with every sunrise. Chances of an afternoon above 50 degrees rise to 40 percent by the end of the week.

The third cold wave of the month arrives on the 9th or 10th, but it is typically one of the mildest so far in the year. Frost strikes the early garden 60 percent of all the nights, however, and there is still a five to 10 percent chance each day this week for a high only in the 20s. Odds of rain or snow are about one in three most days of the period; the 10th is the wettest day with a 50 percent chance of precipitation. But the Sun typically shines a little more than it did last week, with the 14th and the 17th often producing fewer clouds than any time since January 26th through 28th.

Week 3

With equinox, the chances of highs in the 20s fall below 5 percent for the first time since the middle of December, but the 18th usually brings the greatest chance of frost across the Border States in the entire month, a full 90 percent chance. Lunar perigee on the 19th and full Moon on the 20th are almost guaranteed to give a biting edge to Early Spring equinox.

March 20th is typically the wettest day of

the week, with a 60 percent chance of precipitation and the most thunderstorms since autumn. Lunar influence is expected to complement the cold front due near this date with turbulent weather.

The 21st is often the driest day of the week, with just a 25 percent chance of precipitation. The 21st also brings the most Sun of any day in the third week of March: 70 percent of those days are clear to partly cloudy. Only two other March days get so bright, the 7th and the 15th.

Week 4

The last quarter of March brings dramatic changes. For the first time since October 22, there is a 5 percent chance of highs reaching 80 degrees along the 40th Parallel. And on the 31st, those chances double. On the 23rd, the odds for morning frost are about one in two, but on the 29th, those odds fall to just one in four. In the warmest years of all, frost can be gone until October or November (but an average season brings 20 more dawns below the freezing mark).

Through the 28th, cold afternoons in the 30s still happen one year in ten or 15, but then on the 29th and 30th, chances of such cold drop to less than 5 percent for the first time since the end of October. The 25th through the 28th are the driest and sunniest days of the week, each bringing a 60 percent chance or better of a break in the clouds. The 29th is the day most likely to bring overcast conditions; the Sun is absent on that date 65 percent of the time, and rain falls 50 percent of the time.

The likelihood of a thunderstorm is six times

greater this week than it was last week. And tornado season usually begins now and lasts through the summer.

Best Lunar Planting Times
Seed bedding plants in the North and seeds for most hardy vegetables and flowers in the South near the new White Cabbage Butterfly Moon (March 6). Plant root crops and perform animal maintenance under the waning Moon (March 21 – 31).

Calendar of Feast Days and Holidays for Farmers, Gardeners and Homesteaders

March 5, 2019: Mardi Gras The month-long carnival season ends today with a big party and feast before Ash Wednesday and the start of the Lenten fast.

Almanack Literature
Bruce and the Gelding
By Dawn Shovar

In the summer of 1997, I got the idea that I needed to have a few chickens around the place, like Grandma used to have. I decided on Bantams, and it wasn't long until I found a little red rooster I called Bruce and two little red hens, Lucy and Ethel.

Being from a 4-H project and having been shown at the county and state fairs, they were tame and used to being handled. If you wanted to pick them up, they would just lie down on the ground in front of you and you could pick them up and handle them easily.

A couple of months after they settled in, they finally learned that there were really good things outside on the ground to eat. However, about that time came the meeting with the horse.

Poor Bruce! He must have thought the horse walking toward him was a funny looking person, and he lay down in front of the gelding. The result was a broken leg, just above his foot, and below the "chicken leg" part.

I called my vet, and being a good sport, he agreed to try to set the leg. His first question was why didn't I just have Bruce for supper. The next statement was that he wasn't sure how a chicken's foot worked below the "chicken leg" part, but at least he had the good foot to compare it to. He got the leg fixed up with a splint, and after about four rewraps, the leg turned out good as new.

Bruce ended up living a long life and having a lot of chicks, and I still have 14 of his offspring. However, there were no chicks while he was in his splint. Lucy and Ethel wouldn't have anything to do with him!

The Squawk That Saved My New Winter Coat
By Myrna Glass

I have been called a workaholic. I'm afraid that I'll have to admit "guilty as charged." It was all the fault of my mother! She introduced work to me by making it fun!

When I was about six, and my brothers four and eight, she gave us each one square yard of garden. We made the rows, hoed and weeded it. When it was ready, we harvested it. That satisfied the desire of every little kid to say, "I did it all by myself." How proud I was when my mother announced at the table, "Myrna furnished the radishes for dinner."

At about eight years, I advanced to the care of a pen-full of ducks under the care of an old hen. When they were sold, I got all the money.

When I became a teen, I advanced to the care of a brooder house full of half-grown roosters. They ran free all day. In the evening, I'd go down in the field, accompanied by our old collie, to close the coop. The coop had to be closed to keep the night varmints from having them for a midnight snack. I was promised that if I were successful, I would have money for a new winter coat when they were sold.

Since I was a normal teen, somehow the work didn't seem as important as usual. My hormones kicked in, and that cute sophomore looked pretty good to me. It's called "puppy love." Is that because it often leads to a dog's life? Mine didn't, thank heaven!

Anyhow, I had a date on Sunday night. I had a good time, and got home before a big summer storm came.

The next morning, I started the fire in the basement range to heat water to do the family laundry. Then, I remembered my chickens. I had forgotten to shut them in the night before!

As I neared the coop, my dream of a new coat became a nightmare. Oh, no! The coop was surrounded by dozens of my chickens, lying flat on the soggy ground.

I asked myself, "How can I get rid of dozens of chickens? Maybe I could burn them in the range." So, I picked one up, wiped it off with old rags and took him to the basement.

"I know," I thought, "I'll wrap him in newspaper to get him started." As I tried to stuff him into the stove, though, I heard a squawk! Oh, it really was not a squawk, just a feeble "peep," but it was music to my ears.

In fact, I had overreacted. Not only was the squawking rooster alive, but also ALL of the other chickens! And they all lived long enough to help pay for my new coat that was " saved by a squawk."

Bill Felker

THE ALMANACK HOROSCOPE FOR ARIES INTO TAURUS IN APRIL 2019

Beneath the systole and diastole of a starry night,
Iris, allium, the proffered chalices of tulips,
The colors of a fabulous dusk in Tunisia:
All the prayer-wheels of April-into-May luster
Spinning God-drunk – till finally beside
The moon-daft willow, slack as a marionette,
The frenzy of scotch broom,
The fleet-souled orioles marshal, at wolf's hour,
Then sally in one brilliant will.

Cyrus Cassells

The Gregorian Calendar

S	M	T	W	T	F	S
	1	2	3	4	5	6
7	8	9	10	11	12	13
14	15	16	17	18	19	20
21	22	23	24	25	26	27
28	29	30				

Notes on Stability

On February's Cross Quarter Day, the Sun rose between the Danielsons' house and Lil's house across the street. By equinox, the Sun had moved a little further north and rose over just Lil's house. At summer solstice, sunrise will occur in the northwest between Jerry and Lee's house and Lil's.

I use the names of the houses the way I always have for the past thirty-four years, even though their original owners are long gone. To me, the houses are gnomons, or markers with which to measure progress of the Sun. But they do that only from a certain window of my home. Disconnected from my window, they lose their astronomical significance. If I look at Jerry and Lee's house from the corner of Limestone and High Street, I learn nothing about the time of year. If I approach Lil's house from the alley, I would not know anything about my place in the world.

The Trappist monks I know take a vow of stability, a vow to remain with a single community, often a single building, for the rest of their lives. For them, the Sun always rises and sets in relation to the windows of their cloister. The Sun on the chapel walls is a dial of the year and of their lives.

What lessons does that kind of stability bring? What bearings do I need and want? Do I wish to cut myself loose from the landmarks that seem to frame my existence? Or is that kind of stability only an illusion of perspective?

I ruminate and speculate that if I had a compass, I would not need to know where Lil's house was in order to know the season. It would seem that if I had a compass and a map, I could always know where I was. But that is not always the case, either. I would need a starting point. Orienteering always begins from a known location and uses points of control.

So it seems that even though Lil is dead and her house is only due east of my window and not due east of anyone else's window in the world, even though I am the only one who marks Cross Quarter Day with sunrise between her house and the Danielsons' house (and they died long ago, too), it seems to me that without that odd and arbitrary global positioning system, I would be lost.

If I moved away or became disoriented in mind or body, it seems likely that I could only find myself again from some other window on some other street, in the context of some other buildings from which to wait and see the Sun rising through the year, a window from which to see myself.

It also seems to me that I have spent my whole life looking for and through such windows, marking whatever I needed to mark in order to keep my balance; it seems to me now that stability is far more precious than I had thought, and that such a monastic vow, far from being restrictive, may be the window to time and place, and possibly the only window that there is.

The Aries-Taurus Sun

Cross-Quarter Day is April 21, halfway between equinox and solstice, and the Sun enters the Late Spring sign of Taurus on the same date.

The effects of the rising temperatures and longer days under the sign of Aries are always cumulative. Suddenly, the tree line is greening and all the tulips open. Hepatica, periwinkle, toad trillium, cowslip, rue anemone, shepherd's purse, ground ivy, violet and small-flowered buttercup are all in bloom. Although some snow trillium and twinleaf are done flowering, it is budding time for meadow rue, large-flowered trillium, trout lily, Jacob's ladder, bellwort, ragwort and sedum.

Pastures fill with golden winter cress, purple henbit and dandelions. Blossoms appear on the first strawberry plants, and hearts form on the bleeding heart. Asparagus comes up in the sun. Summer's jumpseed and zigzag goldenrod sport four to six leaves apiece. Comfrey and lily-of-the-valley are seven inches high. In the herb garden, wood mint is at least eight inches tall and sweet for tea. Chives are ready for salads.

The earliest grasshoppers and tadpoles swarm from their eggs under the sign of the Aries-Taurus Sun. Tent caterpillars appear in the wild cherry trees. Aphids hatch, and ladybugs come to find them. Small diving water beetles hunt in ponds and sloughs, dragonflies and damselflies hunting above them in the Sun. Water rushes and purple loosestrife, water lilies and pickerel plants have suddenly produced foliage in ponds and wetlands.

Along Nebraska's Platte River, sandhill cranes depart for breeding grounds in the North. In Yellowstone, wood ticks follow the receding snow, and in Montana, Grizzly Bears come out of hibernation.

Phases of the Cows Switching Their Tails Moon

On the morning of April 23 of 2005, Ruby Nicholson (who was 95 at the time) called to tell me how she hadn't seen cows switching their tails since last October, and how she'd been watching all winter and the cows hadn't switched their tails.

But then that morning, she said, she had seen cows standing knee deep in mud, and she saw one of them switch its tail, and that, she declared, was a sign of spring. And so this year's Cows Switching Their Tails Moon is named in memory of Ruby and her keen eye for seasonal changes.

Of course, when cows switch their tails, all kinds of other things are happening. Farmers plant field corn and oats, and gardeners put in sweet corn and lettuce and spinach and potatoes. Under the Cows Switching Their Tails Moon, toads and green frogs sing, ducklings and goslings hatch. Daffodils and grape hyacinths and creeping phlox and wisteria come into flower. Spring beauties and Virginia bluebells fill the hillsides. Cowslip season begins in the wetlands. Flowering pears and plums and apples and cherries bloom and set their fruit.

Past Full Moon and well into Taurus, ginkgo, tree-of-heaven, ash, locust and mulberry spread out new leaves. Mock orange, Korean lilac and honeysuckles announce the most fragrant days of the year.

April 5: The Cabbage White Butterfly Moon becomes the new Cows Switching Their Tails Moon at 3:50 a.m.
The coincidence of New Moon and the second major high-pressure system to cross the nation at the end of April's first week is likely to intensify the low barometric pressure that will occur before the arrival of that front. Since this week of April is a major tornado window of the year, severe storms could well occur.

April 12: The Moon enters its second quarter at 3:06 p.m.
The weakening Moon will favor relatively mild and gentle weather in the second week of the month.

April 16: The Moon reaches perigee (its position closest to Earth) at 5:02 p.m.
Lunar tidal influence swells by April 15, and perigee increases chances of a killing frost throughout the northern half of the United States.

April 19: The Moon is full at 6:12 a.m.
With full Moon so close to perigee, the danger of frost remains high.

April 26: The Moon enters its fourth quarter at 5:18 p.m.
After a chilly middle April, lunar influence finally wanes, favorable for a warm planting period before May.

April 28: The Moon reaches apogee (its position farthest from Earth) at 1:20 p.m.
Apogee typically weakens lunar influence, and the last two weather systems of the month should be gentle and maybe even frost-free.

The Planets

♃ ♄ ♂ ♀

All the major planets remain visible this month, complementing and enhancing the lengthening days and new fauna with their beauty. Rising before midnight in Ophiuchus, Jupiter travels across the morning sky, lying in the southern sky before sunrise.

Coming up after midnight in Sagittarius, Saturn moves along the southern horizon following well behind Jupiter until dawn.

The last of the major planets to appear before sunup, Venus moves retrograde into Aquarius, following Sagittarius and Saturn along the tree line. Now in Taurus, Mars remains the low Evening Star along the western horizon.

The Stars

When the Sun approaches the sign of Taurus in the third week of April, the Big Dipper comes as far as possible into the southern sky, and its pointers (the two outside stars of its dipper cup) are positioned almost exactly north-south after dark. Now Cepheus and Cassiopeia, which were nearly overhead in Early Winter, have moved to the far side of Polaris along the northern horizon.

The Milky Way fills the western horizon as Orion sets just behind the Sun. Now the middle of the heavens are in their prime spring planting position, Castor and Pollux to the west, Leo with its bright Regulus directly overhead, and Arcturus dominating the east.

The Shooting Stars

The Lyrid Meteors are active after midnight between Cygnus and Hercules during the second and third week of April, peaking on April 22 and 23. These shooting stars often appear at the rate of 15 to 25 per hour. The gibbous waning Moon may interfere with meteor watching by brightening the sky.

The S.A.D. Stress Index

April brings the day's length and the chances of mild weather into single digits on the S.A.D. Stress Index. Only the cloud column holds out at March levels, but that is not enough to keep the Index from dipping into the gentle 30s when the Moon enters its second and fourth phases.

Of course, the antidotes for S.A.D. are everywhere when the Sun lies in Aries and Taurus. In fact, the horoscope, that is, the "time watch," for this time of year, cancels out most of the factors that contribute to Seasonal Affective Disorder. To the time watcher, wildflowers easily counteract clouds, and singing birds negate the frost, and leafing trees can compensate for a powerful Moon.

Key for Interpreting the S.A.D. Index:
Totals of 100 to 80: Severe stress
79 to 55: Severe to moderate stress
54 to 40: Moderate stress
39 to 25: Light to moderate stress
24 and below: Light stress

Day	Clouds	Weather	Daylight	Moon	Totals
April 5:	16	11	10	19	56
April 12:	14	10	9	5	38
April 16:	14	9	9	20	52
April 19:	13	8	8	26	55
April 26:	13	7	7	10	37
April 28:	12	7	7	5	31

Peak Activity Times for Creatures

The following traditional guide to lunar position shows when the Moon is above or below the country, and, therefore, the portion of the day or night during which livestock, people, fish and game are typically the most active and the hungriest.

Activity is likely to increase at New Moon (April 5) and perigee (April 15) and full Moon (April 19), especially as the barometer falls in advance of cold fronts near those dates.

Ordinarily, the Moon is most powerful when it is overhead (above your position).

Date	**Above**	**Below**
April 1 – 7:	Midnight to Dawn	Afternoons
April 8 – 14:	Mornings	Evenings
April 15 – 21:	Afternoons	Midnight to Dawn
April 22 – 29:	Evenings	Mornings
April 30 – 31:	Midnight to Dawn	Afternoons

Meteorology
Based on Average Arrival of Weather Systems and the Phases of the Moon

Seven major cold fronts move across the nation in an average April. Snow is possible in Northern areas with the arrival of the first three fronts. **Average dates for the weather systems to reach the Mississippi: April 2, 6, 11, 16, 21, 24 and 28.**

Major storms are most likely to occur on the days between April 1 and 11, and between April 19 and 27. Although the intensity of the high-pressure systems moderates after the 22nd, be alert for frost at least two days after each system pushes through your area.

New Moon on April 5 and lunar perigee on April 16 and full Moon on April 19 are expected to intensify the weather systems near those dates. In general, most precipitation usually occurs during the first two weeks of the month.

Weekly Weather Estimates
Week 1

Two major weather systems, one arriving on the 2nd and another coming in on the 6th, usually dominate the first quarter of April in the Lower Midwest, increasing the chance of precipitation. Snow is most likely to fall on the 3rd, 4th, and 5th. There is a 20 percent chance of a high in the 80s this week, and there is more than a 50 percent chance of an afternoon in the 60s or 70s. Still, the first quarter of the fourth month is its coldest quarter, and with New Moon on the 5th, daily chances of frost remain steady at an average of 40 percent throughout the period.

Week 2

Rain is the rule for April's second quarter. After the third major high-pressure system passes through, however, a brief mid-April dry spell typically occurs on the 11th and 12th, chances of precipitation falling to 25 percent. The 11th is also the brightest day in the first half of April, bringing an 80 percent chance of Sun, the best chances since the 7th of March. As for temperatures, chances of highs below 50 degrees fall to less than 10 percent on the 11th, where they remain until they drop to 5 percent on April 22nd. Milder highs above the 60s occur better than half the time on all the days of this quarter except on the 10th, when cooler conditions typically prevail. Frost strikes an average of 30 percent of the nights.

Week 3

In spite of perigee and the full Moon at the beginning of this period, the chances of a high above 50 degrees are 85 percent on almost every day during April's third quarter, and temperatures above 60 come at least half the time. Cold 20s are rare (just a 5 percent chance on the 17th and 18th), but frost still strikes an average of one night in four. Beginning on the 20th, the chances of an afternoon high in the 70s or 80s jumps from an average of 25 percent way up to 45 percent.

Rain or snow falls an average of 35 percent of the time this week of the year, the 15th, being the wettest day of all, carrying a 45 percent chance of rain and an additional 20 percent chance of snow. Beginning on the 16th of the month, a major increase in the average daily amount of sunlight takes place: a rise from early April's 50/50 chance of Sun or clouds up to a brighter 70 percent chance of clear to partly cloudy conditions.

Week 4

Late Spring arrives this week, the warm weather creating unmistakable markers in the progress of the year. Among those landmarks:

The 26th and the 30th record freezing temperatures less than 5 percent of the time, the first time that has happened since late September.

After the 22nd, chances of snow drop below 5 percent below the 40th Parallel.

Chances of a cold day in the 30s or 40s fall to only 10 percent on the 22nd, then plummet another eight percent on the 26th.

Beginning on April 27th, highs in the 90s become possible, and the chances of a high in the 80s pass the 20 percent mark. The chances of a high above 70 degrees are now 50/50 or better for the first time this year.

April Frostwatch

Between April 1 and June 1, up to dozen frosts occur at lower elevations along the 40th Parallel during a typical year. Of course, in some years, frosts end with March. Normally, however, the approximate chances of frost follow a regular and steadily declining trajectory through the end of May.

Add 10 percent to the figures below for each 100 miles north of the 40th Parallel (or for each 500 feet of elevation above 1,000 feet along that Parallel). Subtract 10 percent for each 100 miles south of the 40th Parallel.

April 1:	95%
April 5:	90%
April 10:	80%
April 15:	70%
April 20:	50%
April 25:	40%
April 30:	30%

The Allergy Index
Estimated April Pollen Count

(On a scale of 0 – 700 grains per cubic meter)
Major pollen source: box elders, maples, pussy willows, flowering crabs and cherries.

April 1: 10	April 10: 50
April 15: 100	April 25: 200

April 30: 400

Estimated April Mold Count
(On a scale of 0 – 7,000 grains per cubic meter)

April 1: 1300
April 5: 1600
April 10: 1700
April 15: 1800
April 20: 1900
April 25: 2000
April 30: 2100

Best Lunar Planting Times

Seed tender plants under lights in the North but plant most vegetables and flowers under the dark of the new Cows Switching Their Tails Moon (April 5). Plant root crops and perform animal maintenance under the waning Moon (April 1-4 or April 20-30).

Calendar of Feast Days and Holidays for Farmers, Gardeners and Homesteaders

April 19 – 27, 2019 Passover: The Jewish market typically is best after religious holidays come to a close. Milk-fed lambs and kids below 60 pounds are favored for the Passover market. Lamb stew is a traditional Seder dish at Passover Seder dinners.

April 1 – June 15, 2019 Dates of the graduation

cookout market

April 14-17, 2019: **New Year's Day** for immigrants from Cambodia, Thailand and Laos. The Asian market often favors animals in the 60 to 80-pound live-weight range.

April 21, 2019: Roman Easter Save your newly weaned, milk-fed lambs weighing about 25 to 45 pounds and not older than three months, for this market. Light-colored meat is best, a sign of the suckling animal. Lambs weighing under 20 pounds or more than 50 pounds may not bring the best price.

April 28, 2019: Orthodox Easter Orthodox Easter animals should also be milk fed. They can be a little bit bigger than the Roman Easter lambs (between 40 and 60 pounds), and should be nice and fat.

Almanack Literature
The Dog with the High IQ
By Ron Hocker

Many of us have owned smart dogs, and many of us farm folks - smart *farm* dogs.

When I was about eight or nine years old, my dad took me to a farm friend of his to do some business. It was almost my birthday. Well, this old guy, Art, had a dog that had just had puppies. He said, "How about a puppy for your birthday?" Dad agreed, and we brought it home. Then came a name for it. I don't remember who it was who picked out

"Micky," but we all agreed.

As my dog grew, we all fell in love with her. We never really knew what breed she was, but I can remember old Art saying it was part collie and something else. Well, she never got to be collie size, maybe half. She went with us to every corner of the farm. Dad even had to build special platforms on the tractors so she could ride if she wanted, and as I remember, she liked that a lot. The older she became, the smarter she got, and without much training.

This dog must have had part of a human brain. All we had to say was we were going blackberry picking and she would bark and wag her tail. She loved to go along, eating any berries that fell to the ground.

The one memory of her I'll never forget was one day in the summer when the sweet corn was ripe, Mother told Dad she planned to put up some corn in the afternoon when we returned from town. So Dad and I took a couple baskets to the sweet corn patch (that was at least 400 yards from the house), and as time was limited that morning, we never had time to get near all of it picked and into the baskets. But most of it was at least pulled and thrown on the ground on the outside of the patch.

We went to town for probably two or three hours, and when we got home, we noticed Micky was sitting by a pile of corn, barking and wagging her tail. In disbelief, Dad inspected a few ears of corn only to find teeth marks and saliva on the husks. Micky had brought all of the remaining corn from the patch to the house while we were gone!

Needless to say, Micky got a special treat that day, and one was a big hug from all of us.

Strutter Gets in Trouble
By Ibbie Ledford

Winter was a relaxing time on the farm in rural West Tennessee. The crops were laid by and most of the work was done until spring, except for feeding the animals and milking the cows. Papa could while away much of his time at Uncle Sam's store playing dominoes.

The week before Thanksgiving, Mama and her sister, Aunt Ibbie, were busy cleaning house and baking pies and cakes. Thanksgiving has always been my favorite holiday. We get to see relatives that we haven't seen in a long time, the food is great, and there are no gifts expected.

One nice sunshiny day our chickens were scratching around pecking at corn that Mama had thrown out or digging up a worm for a treat. Mama and Papa didn't know they were raising "organic" or "free range" chickens as they are called today.

We had an old rooster that year that we called Strutter. He would strut around the back yard, flapping his wings like the whole yard was his domain and would attack anyone he thought was invading it.

One day I was riding my tricycle in his territory. He began following close behind me and just as I rode past the cistern, he jumped toward me. Someone had forgotten to replace the lid on the cistern, so when I ducked down, Strutter flew over me right into the cistern. Luckily, it hadn't rained lately and there was only about a foot of water in it. But Strutter was really flapping and squawking.

I yelled at my older brother, Austin, who was always lying in the hayloft reading a book when there was no work to be done. He came running, lowered the water bucket down, and Strutter grabbed on to it. Austin pulled him up, and Strutter went running, still flapping and squawking.

We had a good laugh at him, and Mama said he would be on our Thanksgiving dinner table. We never had turkey for Thanksgiving since we had all those chickens right in our own back yard.

Bill Felker

THE ALMANACK HOROSCOPE
FOR
TAURUS INTO GEMINI
IN MAY
2019

May I not serve, then, in Thy garden
And in Thy fields and farm,
Stirring the soil around the radishes
And pulling rhubarb by the fence?
Layering the Latham stems to make new growth
For warm sweet berries born two seasons hence?
Setting the tendril feet of runnered plantlets
In crumbled, tendered soil within the row?
Pausing to know the lilac's dearness,
The gentle petaled rose upon my lips,
The lemon balm so sweet on fingertips,
And the sharp, wild scent of catnip cornered there.
Or, tractor mounted, turn the vibrant earth
Warm to the Sun in overlapping layers
Of joy and productivity.
At star shine,
Crimson clover in stretching, wilting rows,
Cut at first bloom to hold all good within.
Quiet in star glow for tomorrow's turning
To tomorrow's sun.

Janet Stevens, *Joy*

The Gregorian Calendar

S	M	T	W	T	F	S
			1	2	3	4
5	6	7	8	9	10	11
12	13	14	15	16	17	18
19	20	21	22	23	24	25
26	27	28	29	30	31	

Higher Time

Keeping a notebook of what happens every day in the small world around me, I often think about the cyclical quality of events in nature. The repeating quality of the sky and the landscape, is something similar to what sociologist Charles Taylor describes as "Higher Time" (as opposed to linear, "Secular Time") in *A Secular Age,* his study of the rise of Humanism.

In Secular Time, says Taylor, "one thing happens after another, and when something is past, it's past." Higher Time, on the other hand, dramatizes cycles like those represented in the Christian liturgical calendar or in the repeating nature of the year. And even though the modern world seems to do business completely in Secular Time, the alternate viewpoint persists and may even be dominant inside memory.

Memory Time is always Higher Time. Not only does memory retain a whole impression of experience, but it also blends, erases, and re-sequences pieces of the past, allowing the feasts of birth and death, love and disappointment to return, mellow or fester, winnowed to their core.

So too with observation of the natural year, the repetition of the seasons within the mind mixes and combines the years, unifies them and reevaluates them, distortions showing the selective power of emotion and insight over linear statistics.

To withdraw from Secular Time is to come home to a centered self where experiences are sifted and unified and made whole to return again. Like a book of days, the mind recollects choices and destinies, showing and combining in the radii of its vortex the higher shadows and auras of repeating Suns.

The Taurus-Gemini Sun

On May 9, the Taurus Sun reaches three-fourths of the way to solstice. It enters the Early Summer sign of Gemini on May 21, marking the high solar tide of the year throughout the Northern Hemisphere.

Riding the tide of the Sun, mulberry season

begins for both the red and white varieties, and it typically lasts until the end of Early Summer – good for birds and good for pies! Tea roses and achillea open in the garden, and the first foxtail grass ripples by the side of the road. Asiatic lilies, poison ivy, meadow rue, Indian hemp, and the catalpa trees are budding.

July's wild petunia foliage is a foot tall. August's boneset has grown knee high. Canadian geese are molting, now that all of their goslings have hatched. Mother grackles and robins are cleaning their nests, often depositing the white droppings of their babies in your birdbath or pond.

The time of Taurus-into-Gemini is high time for insects: time to check the cucumbers for cucumber beetles, the alfalfa for potato leafhoppers, and the roses for mites. Chinch bugs hatch in the lawn. Whiteflies attack azaleas. Weevils assault the yellow poplars. Leafminers work arborvitae, birch, locusts, boxwood, elms, holly and juniper. Inspired by all the insects, weaving spiders weave the first major network of cobwebs across the woodland paths. Wolf spiders hunt the fields and forest floors. Birds feast and feed their young.

Across the lower Midwest, there are hedges of white elderberry flowers, roadsides of violet crown vetch, great fields of golden wheat. If you follow the Ohio Valley south, you will find hemlocks gone to seed near Louisville, teasel blooming. Vibrant orange butterfly weed has opened in southern Illinois.

All June's thistles are decaying below St. Louis, and cattails have their pollen. Sweet clover has almost disappeared by Nashville, and the blackberries are turning a little red. Below Memphis, Queen Anne's lace blooms, wild lettuce and horseweed, too, and elderberries set their fruit.

The wheat fields are bare in the Gulf States, the roadsides full of black-eyed Susans, pennywort, thin-leafed mountain mint, Mexican hat. And the sugar cane crop, thousands of miles away in Belize, paces the sweet corn in the Ohio Valley.

The Phases of the Golden Buttercup Moon

Middle Spring folds into Late Spring under the Golden Buttercup Moon. Sweet clover, parsnips and wild lettuce are already a foot high, waterleaf and sweet rockets have buds, white spring cress opens, locust and grape vines are leafing.

Garden chives bloom as the first tall grass heads up under the New Moon. Black walnut trees leaf out and the green ash trees blossom while the maple flowers collapse all at once. Pussy willow leaves race with the box elders, both about half size.

Rue anemone, Jack-in-the-pulpit, toothwort and large-flowered trilliums are in full bloom, early meadow rue and ragwort and bellwort almost ready, wild phlox budding, too, under the waxing Moon. Ginger leaves have unfolded from the ground. Spring beauties fill the lawns. All the grasses in town and country take on exciting vibrancy, glow with life, as though their usually invisible aura could no longer be contained and took to shining.

Tadpoles have left the safety of their eggs and have gone out one by one to explore their ponds. Red-winged blackbirds build nests and sing on fences all the way from Alaska to the Gulf of Mexico. Some orchard grass and rye are ready to harvest. Bluegrass is budding. It is viburnum season and buckeye flower time. Last year's catalpa seedpods fall in late Taurus thunderstorms.

Waning through Gemini, the Moon brings the time of flowering fruit trees to a close. The Great Dandelion Bloom that began in February across the South now reaches the Canadian border and then turns gray and fragile. All the gold has disappeared from Middle Spring's forsythia as daisies bud, and ferns unravel. The six-petaled white star of Bethlehem says it's May in the city, and the four-petaled pink and purple sweet rockets tell the time of year throughout the pastures.

Lilies of the valley have their bells, and the first bright yellow cressleaf groundsel opens in wetlands. Rhubarb pies grow everywhere as the first strawberry flowers, as Virginia creepers get their new shiny leaves, as azaleas brighten and as honeysuckle leaves turn the undergrowth deep May green.

The high leaf canopy casts the first shade on the flower and vegetable garden under the waning

Golden Buttercup Moon, and the first great wave of songbirds reaches Lake Erie, dominated by the white-throated sparrow, ruby-crowned kinglet, yellow-rumped warbler, black-and-white warbler, palm warbler, Nashville warbler, swamp sparrow and hermit thrush.

May 4: The Buttercup Moon is New at 5:45 p.m.
This New Moon increases chances of frost above the 40th Parallel. Then lunar influence weakens until the approach of perigee.

May 11: The Moon enters its second quarter at 8:12 p.m.

May 13: The Moon reaches perigee (its position closest to Earth) at 4:53 p.m.
Lunar perigee is likely to strengthen the cold front due between May 10 and 15. Be ready to protect tender plantings from frost.

May 18: The Moon is full at 4:11 p.m.
This full Moon presents a major chance of frost in northern states, but as the Moon wanes, lunar conditions favor warm, stable weather until the approach of June.

May 26: The Moon reaches apogee (its position farthest from Earth) at 8:27 a.m. and enters its final quarter at 11:34 a.m.

The Planets

♃ ♄ ♂ ♀

Moving retrograde again, this time into Pisces, Venus remains the huge Morning Star in the east before dawn. Jupiter is in Ophiuchus, rises in the east after sundown and traverses the sky throughout the night, arriving in the southwest before sunrise.

Mars, following Taurus into the sunset, may be visible as the red Evening Star, or, just before sunrise you may glimpse it in the east far below Venus.

Rising from the southeast before midnight in Sagittarius, Saturn travels through the night until it disappears near dawn.

The Stars

Cassiopeia and the Milky Way lie on the northern horizon before midnight. Cygnus rises from the northeast, Ophiuchus from the east, Sagittarius and Libra from the southeast. Centaurus and Corvus are low on the southern horizon. Hydra snakes across the southwest. Monoceros is setting in the west, Gemini going down due west, Capella and Perseus disappearing into the northwest.

The Shooting Stars

The Eta Aquarids are active from April 18 through May 28, with the most meteors expected on May 5. The Moon is not expected to interfere with meteor watching.

Peak Activity Times for Creatures

The following traditional guide to lunar position shows when the Moon is above or below the country, and, therefore, the portion of the day or night during which livestock, people, fish and game are typically the most active and the hungriest.

Activity is likely to increase at New Moon (May 4) and perigee (May 13) and full Moon (May 18), especially as the barometer falls in advance of cold fronts near those dates.

Ordinarily, the Moon is most powerful when it is overhead (above your position).

Date	Above	Below
May 1 – 3 :	Mornings	Evenings
May 4 – 10:	Afternoons	Midnight to Dawn
May 11 – 17:	Evenings	Mornings
May 18 – 25:	Midnight to Dawn	Afternoons
May 26 – 31 :	Mornings	Evenings

Meteorology
Based on Average Arrival of Weather Systems and the Phases of the Moon

The cold fronts of Late Spring usually cross the Mississippi on or about **May 2, 7, 12, 15, 21, 24 and 29.** Tornadoes, floods or prolonged periods of soggy pasture are most likely to occur within the following windows: May 3-12 and May 17-24. The last days of May and the first week of June are often soaked by the Strawberry Rains.

New Moon on May 4, lunar perigee on May 13 and full Moon on May 18 could contribute to unseasonable cold and to unstable weather.

Weekly Weather Estimates
Week 1

The first quarter of May brings highs above 60 on 75 percent of the afternoons, and warm 70s or 80s a little more than half the years. May 2 is typically the coldest day of the period, bringing cool 50s on 35 percent of the afternoons, and a 20 percent chance of 70s or 80s.

Frost occurs only 10 to 20 percent of the mornings and is most likely after the first high pressure system of the month passes through under the New Moon the 2nd of the month, and after the second system arrives near the 7th.

Each day of the period carries at least a 30 to 35 percent chance of a shower, but some of those days have a much better chance of Sun than others. The 6th has an unusual 95 percent chance of clear to partly cloudy skies, making it historically one of only a handful of such days in the year. The 8th through the 10th are not all that far behind, each having an 80 to 85 percent chance of Sun.

Week 2

An average day in May's second quarter brings rain 25 to 40 percent of the time. The 8th, 11th and the 13th are likely to be the driest of the week, the 12th and 14th the wettest. Typical highs almost always reach above 60 degrees after the 10th of May, and they rise to 70 or above at least 60 percent of the afternoons. May 11th is the day with the warmest weather history of the month: a full 50 percent of May 11ths bring temperatures in the 80s, something which doesn't happen again until the first of June. Also after the 10th of May, the chances of a killing frost drop below 5 percent at average elevations along the 40th Parallel.

Week 3

High temperatures are usually above 60 degrees the week ahead, with the chances of 70s or better rising to 70 percent, a 10 percent increase over last week's chances. A high in the 50s occurs rarely, but if it does appear, it is typically on the 21st and 24th. Chances of frost are low, but tender plants are in some danger after the passage of May's fourth cold front on the 15th and fifth cold front on the 20th, especially at full Moon. The 18th, 19th, and 22nd are the wettest days in the period; the 20th and the 21st are the least likely to bring precipitation.

Week 4

The final week of May is typically a wet one, with completely overcast conditions more common than during any other time of the month. On the 25th, 26th and 27th rain falls almost half the time, and the 29th is one of the rainiest days in the whole year. Average temperature distribution for this time of the month is as follows: 5 percent chance of highs in the 90s, 30 percent for 80s, 30 percent for 70s, 25 percent for 60s, and 10 percent for 50s. The brightest days of the week are usually the 27th and 30th.

Frostwatch

Between May 1 and June 1, only a few mornings of light frost occur at average elevations along the 40th Parallel. Chances of freezing temperatures after the dates listed below are:

May 1:	45 percent
May 5:	35 percent
May 10:	25 percent
May 15:	15 percent
May 20:	10 percent
May 25:	5 percent
May 31:	2 percent

The Allergy Index
Estimated May Pollen Count

(On a scale of 0 - 700 grains per cubic meter)
Pollen from flowering trees usually peaks about the 10th of May, but trees continue to be the major source of pollen in the air until grass pollen replaces it in the third week of the month.

May 1: 400   May 5: 540   May 10: 500
May 20: 250   May 25: 160   May 31: 100

Estimated May Mold Count

(On a scale of 0 - 7,000 grains per cubic meter)
May 1: 2600   May 5: 3000   May 10: 2000
May 15:1100   May 20: 250   May 25: 150
May 31: 100

Best Lunar Planting Times

Put in root crops during the first four days of the month, and then plant everything from soybeans to tender tomatoes and impatiens as the Golden Buttercup Moon waxes during the first part of the month. Throughout this period, weather is more important than lunar position or phase, so do as much field and garden work as you can when you can.

The S.A.D. Stress Index

May brings an easing of Seasonal Affective Disorder for the majority of people in the Northern Hemisphere. The summer-like day's length, the mild weather of Middle Spring, and the gradually decreasing cloud cover, contribute to the start of the least stressful period of the year. The S.A.D. Index reflects these changes, dipping to 19 by May 26.

Key for Interpreting the S.A.D. Index:
Totals of 100 to 80: Severe stress
79 to 55: Severe to moderate stress
54 to 40: Moderate stress
39 to 25: Light to moderate stress
24 and below: Light stress

Day	Clouds	Weather	Daylight	Moon	Totals
May 4:	10	5	6	20	41
May 11:	10	4	5	10	29
May 13:	9	5	4	20	38
May 18:	9	8	4	25	46
May 26:	8	8	3	0	19

Calendar of Feast Days and Holidays for Farmers, Gardeners and Homesteaders

May 6, 2019: Ramadan begins at sunset. Advertise your lambs and kids in preparation for the end of Ramadan on June 5.

Almanack Literature
The Escape Artist
By Richard Dietke

Star Eyes, a Romney wether (neutered male sheep), lives on our farm in Central West Virginia, with several other sheep born on this farm. A bottle baby, he spent much of his time in the barn with the horses and goats. As he grew into a very large sheep, we soon discovered that he could open the stall door by himself.

On several occasions when he was put into a stall with other sheep in the barn, we could come back later to find them all eating hay in the barn aisle. With each of us blaming the other for not sliding the stall door catch shut. Then one day we decided to watch them. After a couple of minutes, Star Eyes went to the door, stuck his tongue into the hand hole cutout in the door catch and slid it open by turning his head.

Our conclusion was that he learned to do this from our horse, Whiskey, because the horse would do this and we would have to tie his stall door to keep him in at night.

Boss To The Rescue
By Ann Witte

Beardies are fairly soft natured yet their bravery surfaces when it is needed. Boss was one of those typical Beardies who proved his courage in many ways, but in one particular way for me.

I had put our four-horned Jacob ram, a very hateful and nasty ram, at that, in with three wethers so he had some company. One day I noticed that one of the wethers had a messy rear that had dried and thus needed to be trimmed off. The sheep had gone behind the shed in a three-to-four-foot-wide alleyway to stay in the shade. As usual, I had Boss along to help with all the sheepwork for the day.

Without thinking at all, I went into that narrow area to get the wether; Boss tagged along. Before I knew it, the ram had appeared and, lowering his head, rushed directly at me. The next thing happened faster than reading will tell. Boss jumped ahead of me to stop the ram; he took the hard blow that was intended for me! The dog cried out but still managed to bite the ram, which backed the sheep off.

A quick trip to the vet and a couple of X-rays later, Boss was said to have three broken ribs and a bruised heart and lung. He spent the next six weeks in a rib wrap. There is no way to cast ribs, but he insisted on accompanying me after four weeks, so we went together. I didn't have him do much work; I doubt he cared. Being a very dark grey and nearly markingless Beardie, the white rib wrap sure was obvious; his courage was not.

Bill Felker

THE ALMANACK HOROSCOPE
FOR
GEMINI INTO CANCER
IN JUNE
2019

There is in all things an inexhaustible sweetness and purity, a silence that is a fount of action and joy. It rises up in wordless gentleness and flows out to me from the unseen roots of all created being, welcoming me tenderly, saluting me with indescribable humility.

Thomas Merton

The Gregorian Calendar

S	M	T	W	T	F	S
						1
2	3	4	5	6	7	8
9	10	11	12	13	14	15
16	17	18	19	20	21	22
23	24	25	26	27	28	29
30						

Autobiography
Horas non numero nisi serenas. (I only count the hours that are happy.)
Horas non numero nisi aestivas. (I only count the summer hours.)

Latin Sundial Inscriptions

I often think about a notebook Diana loaned me decades ago, the diary of A. J. Kiser, a local man who wrote a little about his life on almost every day between September 1950 and December 1952.

The journal entries placed weather statistics and baseball scores side by side with phrases about marriages, anniversaries, election results, births, deaths, fishing and digging for worms. I assume that some of these things were more important to him than others, but the diary gives no clues, recording events with lean sentences, all of equal brevity and style.

I am partial to weather recorders and list makers and journal keepers. I feel a kinship with them, especially when I read their notes, which were perhaps not meant to be read by another person, not meant to be shared but rather to help the author keep track of his or her own life, or some particular part of it that had no scaffolding.

I wonder if their notes are really filled with secret codes that hide feelings behind plain statements about ordinary things. Believing that no one writes down an insignificant event, and that recording one event is really about recording something else, I look for clues in Kiser's journal. But the reasons for his selection of apparently unconnected events are hidden between his lines.

Sundial inscriptions about happy and summer hours seem like such good thoughts. I often try to remember only the summer hours, the hours that were happy. I rarely dwell on them too long, however. Instead, those hours appear and disappear and are mixed up like the entries in Kiser's journal, sometimes memories about death and about flowers and about childhood and about children and about my years in North Carolina and about the best love of all and about the time I got caught cheating on my French test and about the afternoon I almost lost a jeep to the river in the badlands beyond Riomar.

Instead of writing such an autobiography, I choose the code: to count the number of lilies in bloom today, to record what butterflies I've seen in the garden and the time the birds wake in the morning and when the crickets sing in the alley behind my house.

The Gemini-Cancer Sun

Summer solstice occurs on June 21 at 10:54 a.m., the Sun entering the Deep Summer sign of Cancer at the same time. Between June 19 and 23, the Sun holds steady at its solstice declination of 23 degrees 26 minutes, and the day's length remains virtually unchanged.

Inside the four common seasonal categories lie clusters of hidden parallel and interlocking seasons that measure and define time inside of time, creating by their colors and shapes and sounds and tastes and smells the broader temporal landscapes. Like the star groups that lie close to the ecliptic, the Earth's phenomena are only limited by what is visible at any time and to any person. Each land star is a season, a galaxy in itself.

The final floral and faunal constellations of the Sun's residence under the sign of Gemini collect fragments of Late Spring and Early Summer, foretell Deep Summer and the sign of Cancer, as well. Late May's clovers still color pastures and lawns. Meadow goat's beard and chicory stand by the roads. The first wild daisies give way to Shasta daisies that last through July. Gaunt yuccas compete with new great mulleins. Common fleabane cedes to daisy fleabane.

The orange day lilies (ditch lilies) are the crown of June, easy transitions to the Asiatic and Oriental lilies and the multicolored day lilies that bloom under the Dog Star, Sirius. Pink spirea and an assortment of hydrangeas last beyond the longest days. Lizard's tail dips to the rivers and ponds. The compass plant follows the Sun, spreading its blossoms above the nettles.

All these plants are glimpses of a homely galaxy as well as reminders of what is not visible or is not noticed. A land star metaphor is less a distortion than a suggestion about an astronomy at hand and an astrology of place. As above, so below. As below, so above.

Phases of the Milkweed Beetle Mating Moon

Beneath the Milkweed Beetle Mating Moon what might seem at first to just be "summer' or the "Dog Days" becomes a spatial-temporal window of milkweed blossoms, paradise of aroma and flavor for the sluggish mating milkweed beetles.

For the elderberry watcher, dreaming of wine and jam, the pale elderberry flower umbels darken into berries and promises of sweet harvests.

Gigantic cecropia moths emerge for love in the dark, their allotted time only a week or two to mate.

The small Canadian thistles that blossomed pink under the Early Summer sign of Gemini, suddenly become thistledown in the wind when the Sun comes into Cancer.

The winter wheat, planted nine months ago, becomes golden and then deep chocolate brown and ready for harvest.

Through all of this, the milkweed beetles find

and hold their mates, oblivious (perhaps) to all the countless capsule-seasons, more than anyone might imagine: Monarch Butterfly Caterpillar Season, Enchanter's Nightshade Season, Black-Eyed Susan Season, Butterfly Weed Season, Cattail Blooming Season and more and more and more, one for every species in its chosen habitat, offering unlimited divisions of passage and change.

June 3: The Milkweed Beetle Mating Moon is new at 10:02 a.m.
The New Moon is likely to strengthen the June 2 cold front, increasing chances of frost in northern states.

June 7: The Moon reaches perigee at 6:21 p.m.
The effects of lunar perigee should be softened by the Moon, which usually has less meteorological effect near entry into its second and fourth quarter.

June 10: The Moon enters its second quarter at 12:59 a.m.

June 17: The Moon is full at 3:31 a.m.
Thunderstorms are likely as Moon influences the June 15 weather system. Chances of hurricane formation increase.

June 23: The Moon is at apogee at 2:50 a.m.
After full Moon, lunar influence on weather and emotions will decline for the rest of the month.

June 25: The Moon enters its final quarter at 4:46 a.m.
Lunar influence continues low until New Moon time approaches once again in early July.

The Planets

♃ ♄ ♂ ♀

Now in Taurus, Venus lies almost due east just before dawn as the huge Morning Star.

Mars rises well after Venus from the east in Gemini, traverses the Gemini sky during the daylight, arriving in the west as the red Evening Star.

After sundown, find Jupiter rising from the southeast in Ophiuchus this month, setting into the western horizon just as Venus appears from the east in Gemini in the morning.

Up early in the evening, Saturn moves with Sagittarius along the southern horizon until it is lost in the dawn.

The Stars

Traveling in Gemini throughout the day, the Sun's declination increases in height above the horizon until it reaches equinox and enters the astrological sign of Cancer on the 21st. Obscured by daylight, the constellations that accompany Gemini during the day include Orion in the middle of the southern sky at noon, the potent Dog Star, Sirius, low behind him, Pisces in the west, Leo in the east, Draco in the north.

Even though these star groups that cluster around the Sun in Gemini may be invisible throughout the days of June, the landscape offers markers that reveal the sky map hidden in the light of the longest days of the year.

The orange ditch lilies, accompanied by thistles and sweet clover, track the stellar course, bookending the solar passage of Early Summer, beginning their flowering a week or so after the Sun leaves the sign of Taurus for Gemini, coming to full bloom just before equinox and then ceding to the easy markers of July, the white Queen Anne's lace and the yellow black-eyed Susans that dominate the roadsides well into Leo and the Dog Days of Deep Summer.

Peak Activity Times for Creatures

The following traditional guide to lunar position shows when the Moon is above or below the country, and, therefore, the portion of the day or night during which livestock, people, fish and game are typically the most active and the hungriest.

Activity is likely to increase at New Moon (June 3) and perigee (June 7) and full Moon (June 17), especially as the barometer falls in advance of cold fronts near those dates.

Ordinarily, the Moon is most powerful when it is overhead (above your position).

Date	Above	Below
June 1 – 2:	Mornings	Evenings
June 3 – 10:	Afternoons	Midnight to Dawn
June 11 – 16:	Evenings	Mornings
June 17 – 24:	Midnight to Dawn	Afternoons
June 25 – 30:	Mornings	Evenings

Meteorology
Based on Average Arrival of Weather Systems and the Phases of the Moon

The cool fronts associated with Early Summer typically cross the Mississippi on or about June 2, 6, 10, 15, 23 and 29. Major storms are most likely to occur on the days between June 5-8, June 13-16 and June 24-28.

New Moon on June 3 (followed by perigee on the 7th) increases the chances of freezing temperatures along the Canadian border and at higher elevations. Full Moon on June 17 could contribute to unstable meteorological conditions in conjunction with the June 15 cool front and contribute to the formation of an early hurricane.

Weekly Weather Estimates
Week 1

The first week of June brings an end to the likelihood of highs in the 50s and 60s at average elevations along the 40th Parallel. Chances of that kind of cold were around 30 percent last week; this week chances of 60s fall to only 15 percent, and 50s are rare.

Temperatures for the days of this week rise into the 70s on 35 percent of the afternoons, into the 80s on 40 percent, and into the 90s on 10 percent. After June 6th, the likelihood of highs reaching into the 90s jumps to 20 percent, and reaches 35 percent by the middle of the month. About 15 percent of the nights bring temperatures in the 30s or 40s.

Rainfall is usually lighter this week than last, and the Sun shines more. Still, showers fall about 40 percent of the time each day, and New Moon on the 3rd and perigee on the 7th are likely to trigger showers or storms.

Week 2

The second week of June always brings an increase in the likelihood of highs in the 90s, and the average percentage of afternoons in the 80s rises above the average percentage for 70s for the first time in the year. Highs in the cold 60s are rare, occurring just 5 percent of the days.

This week also brings more sunshine than almost any other week so far in the year: 85 percent of the days have at least partly cloudy skies. And the week also contains the second-driest day of the month, June 10, which brings a shower only 10 percent of the years. The 13th and 14th are also usually dry, both having just a 20 percent chance of rain. The wettest days in the period are June 8, 9, 11 and 12, each having a 40 percent chance of rain. Between June 8th and 11th, the average temperature rise slows to one degree in four days instead of Late Spring's one degree in three. Then, between the 15th to the 19th, it climbs just one degree in five days, reaching its summer zenith.

Week 3

This period often brings at least four days that historically are favorable for field work. Chances of completely overcast conditions decline to less than 20 percent. Ordinarily, the 16th, 17th, and 18th have a very low incidence of rainfall (just 25 percent chance of showers), but full Moon on the 17th dramatically increase the likelihood of storms.

Temperatures are usually warm, with only 35 percent of the afternoon highs remaining below 80 degrees. Hot 90s occur at least 20 percent of the time. Lows are in the 60s the majority of nights, but 50s and 40s occur up to 40 percent of the time.

Week 4

Sunny skies are the rule for the last week of June: clouds dominate only about 20 percent of all the days, and that makes this period one of the brighter ones in the whole year. Daily chances of rain throughout this period of the month are 30 percent except on the 25th and 26th; those two days are some of the driest of the entire year, carrying only a 15 percent chance of precipitation. High temperatures rise into the 80s at least 60 percent of all the afternoons and climb above 90 on 20 percent of the days. Cooler conditions in the 70s or even the 60s are most likely to occur on the 23rd and 24th.

The S.A.D. Stress Index

Unless the weather is unseasonably hot, few people suffer from S.A.D. in June. The Index reveals a rare window in the year during which astronomical and meteorological factors that cause stress are reduced to almost nothing. The lush growth and flowering of Early Summer easily counters the influence of the Moon.

Key for Interpreting the S.A.D. Index:
Totals of 100 to 80: Severe stress
79 to 55: Severe to moderate stress
54 to 40: Moderate stress
39 to 25: Light to moderate stress
24 and below: Light stress

Day	Clouds	Weather	Daylight	Moon	Total
June 3:	4	4	0	10	18
June 7:	3	2	0	20	25
June 17:	2	2	0	25	29
June 23:	0	0	0	3	3
June 25:	3	5	0	5	13

Best Lunar Planting Times

Under the dark Moon of the first days of the month, continue planting every seed you want to flower or produce fruit during July, August and September. In just one month, it will be time to set out sets of cabbage, collards and kale for harvest from October into Early Winter.

Calendar of Feast Days and Holidays for Farmers, Gardeners and Homesteaders

June 5, 2019: Eid al-Fitr The Festival of the breaking of the Ramadan Fast: Sheep for this market should not be older than a year. Castrated or uncastrated males are acceptable, as are ewes. The best weight for Ramadan sheep is around 60 pounds, but weaned lambs between 45 and 115 pounds are often used. In reviewing your culling program, consider that older sheep often command higher prices during this period.

June 16 , 2019: Father's Day

Almanack Literature
A Timely Revelation
by Alonso Byrd

It was not so long ago that I ran across the following note in a local paper from 1845:

"To ascertain the length of the day and the night at any time of year, double the time of the Sun's rising, which gives the length of the night, and double the time of setting, which gives the length of the day."

On the surface, the quotation seemed innocent enough, and since it appeared to offer a quick and easy method for calculating the day's length, I jotted it down in my notebook.

Before presenting this facile formula to the public, however, I did feel obligated to see just how well it worked.

I began with statistics from January 1. Sunrise time is about 8:00 a.m. According to the formula, you double that time to get the length of the night. All right 8 x 2 = 16. Fine: so the night is 16 hours long. Then I went to Sunset time, which is approximately 5:00 p.m. And 5 x 2 = 10. OK: that makes 10 hours of daylight.

I did some further spot-checking with other dates. The unnerving logical conclusion was that the actual length of the day in 1845 was 26 hours!

When I combined this information with a number of nineteenth-century newspaper reports concerning crocodiles being found in northern rivers, the truth began to surface: One hundred and fifty years ago, North America was a tropical jungle. Heated by a day almost 10 percent longer than we now experience, the region produced lush flora and unexpected fauna.

But as trees were cut down, the Earth's orbit changed, and the days began to shorten to what they are today. Tropical wildlife died off quickly in a period of such radical environmental change; fossils aged with unbelievable alacrity, and vegetation took on a more modern appearance.

While scientists and historians suppressed all this business for their own purposes, machines began to take over some of the backbreaking labor that filled the old day. Progress filled the gap created by the shrinking hours. Automobiles cut the time required to travel from one place to the next. Home appliances abbreviated household drudgery. The workweek shortened.

"The days go by more quickly now," the old folks said, and people thought it was just age, accelerating their sense of passage. Blinded by modernity, no one saw the seconds disappear one by one.

Speaking with Mice II
By Janet Stevens

I was in Guatemala that winter. Most of the disaster from the earthquake was cleaned up, and gardens were planted.

I rented a paneled-off portion of the porch of a grandmother's house in the compound with her son's place. There was space for a narrow bed, a tiny work table and chair, and a bedside table for my lamp and minute hotplate. Water facilities were curtained off on another part of the porch. I had vegetables from the garden. A great purple bougainvillea vine climbed a tree by the mud wall at the edge of the compound. All of this was in walking distance of the market, the language school, and the holy places.

That night, I learned that mice had set up their home in the space between the panels and the old wall. They were there first, took precedence, and frolicked all night long, ever so noisy.

Every night for some time, the mice kept up their clatter in the wall. I stood it for a while. Then, in the middle of a weary night, I thought-spoke to them: "Mice, I am glad you have happy homes here, but I can't rest with you raising the dickens all night. I sure would appreciate it if you could do your noise things when I am awake or away." (They understood thought, but not English.)

I gave it no further thought, and rejoiced in the quiet nights. Then I went up to Panahachel for a few days. The first night home, the racket started again.

"MICE...." I said sternly. Immediate silence. Quiet nights all the rest of the winter there.

THE ALMANACK HOROSCOPE
FOR
CANCER INTO LEO
IN JULY
2019

*Midsummer pause
between the birdsong of Early Spring and Early
Summer
and the insect chorus of Deep and Late Summer:
I wait in this quiet space
as the pull of the Sun reaches its limit,
balances on the edge of this week of the year,
then breaks apart,
folds to the darkening foliage
and the fallen strata of May and June.
I look for cheer in old details,
list the history of events around me,
coming to terms with loss in its teaching:
The cycles are bound together,
closed and tight, the history says;
whatever is taken comes again;
nothing leaves or is left behind.*

bf

The Gregorian Calendar

S	M	T	W	T	F	S
	1	2	3	4	5	6
7	8	9	10	11	12	13
14	15	16	17	18	19	20
21	22	23	24	25	26	27
28	29	30	31			

Backyard Solar Eclipse
As above, so below.
The Emerald Tablet of Hermes Trismegistus

Early in the afternoon of the solar eclipse, I was cutting zinnias, removing the older blossoms to encourage the plants to produce new flowers.

Sparrows chirped off and on and cicadas buzzed and cardinals and crows called once in a while. High clouds sometimes filtered the sunlight, but the day was bright and mild.

A friend had called the day before. He said he had heard that birds stopped singing in the middle of a solar eclipse as though they thought night had arrived and that when the Sun came through the Moon again, the birds resumed their calls.

As the eclipse progressed, the dense honeysuckles and the high locusts and hackberries and Osage that surrounded the yard took on an amber glow. It was not a vision of September so much as a transfiguration to a new sepia season, a thin burnished time far from the decay of autumn.

Then I noticed the cicadas were quiet, and I heard no birds. While I stood surrounded by zinnias, bright red became deep blood-red, yellow became gold, orange became sienna, pink became violet, violet turned purple, bright white was soft and creamy.

And toward the end of it all, as the filter of the eclipse was weakening, two monarch butterflies (which had been so rare this summer) suddenly appeared from over the trees, soared majestically into the yard and floated beside me among the zinnias.

Then one of the monarchs rose high, then swooped toward the other as though he could not hold back, and his consort rose steeply to meet him, and they spun in rapturous encounter, swirling up and around and across the flowers in tight randori.

Then they returned to visiting the flowers where I stood until everything became the way it once had been, and then they flew south over the house together. Cicadas buzzed again. Sparrows chirped. A cardinal sang. Towards the west end of town, crows called out.

The Cancer -Leo Sun

Infinite numbers, delicacies, smells,
With hues on hues expression cannot paint,
The breath of Nature and her endless bloom....

James Thomson

At 3:00 p.m. on July 3, the Earth reaches aphelion, the point at which it is about 153 million kilometers (its greatest distance) from the Sun. Aphelion occurs almost exactly six months from perihelion, Earth's position closest to the Sun (about 148 million kilometers).

Throughout the woods, the blossoms of aphelion reflect the sky: great Indian plantain, avens, honewort, wood nettle, wood mint, lopseed, black-eyed Susans, pokeweed, hobblebush, thimble plant, milkweed, Deptford pink.

By the time the Sun enters its Late-Summer sign of Leo on July 23, leafturn is beginning in the undergrowth. A few yellowing leaves appear on cottonwoods. Angelica blanches in the sun, turns creamy white and pink. Ramps go to seed, and euonymus berries fatten like the honeysuckle berries.

In ponds and wetlands, purple loosestrife

overruns the sloughs, while the heads of lizard's tail, still white and soft a few days ago, become stiff and gray. June's clovers and grasses are past their prime, white and red clover browning in the heat, yellow and white sweet clover spindly and bare. Along the highways, hemlock, parsnips and dock are withered and brittle, ending their chapter of Early Summer.

Balancing loss: a rich cornucopia of color and texture and scent. Among the many flowers blooming in fields and gardens under the Cancer-Leo Sun, find showy coneflowers, phlox, midseason hosta, pale blue campanulas, purple coneflowers, bee balm, germander, skullcap, fogfruit, great Indian plantain, fringed loosestrife, bouncing bets, daisy fleabane, moth mullein, wood mint, tall bell flower, great mullein, small-flowered agrimony, tick trefoil, velvetleaf, trumpet creeper, rose of Sharon and jimson weed.

Phases of the Finches in the Thistledown Moon and the Black Walnut Leafdrop Moon

Consorting with the Cancer-Leo Sun, the Finches in the Thistle Down Moon turns all the nodding Canadian and bull thistles to down, and golden finches haunt the fields to feed. Tree frogs cling to windows, singing through the night.

Early morning birdsong weakens under the Finches in the Thistledown Moon, and the robin predawn chorus comes to a close, the silence pushing the narrative of Deep Summer toward cicadas in the days, crickets and katydids after dark. Woolly bear caterpillars, outriders of October, appear on the warm country roads. Blackberries redden.

Black walnuts are autumn size. Acorns are as big as marbles. Sumac staghorns are velvety red. Catalpa beans grow long and firm. Black raspberries disappear, while the second crop of red raspberries ripens. Osage fruits are bigger than apples.

July 2: The Finches in the Thistle Down Moon is new at 2:16 p.m.
Expect the Corn Tassel Rains to increase as New Moon and lunar perigee cluster during the first four days of the month and stir up turbulence in advance of the July 6 cool front.

July 4: The Moon reaches perigee, its position closest to Earth.
As the Moon moves toward its second quarter, its effect on Earth lessens.

July 9: The Moon enters its second quarter at 5:55 a.m.

July 15: The Moon is full at 4:21 p.m.
This full Moon strengthens the mid-July high-

pressure system, but after that system passes through, lunar position favors stability until the Moon turns new.

July 21: The Moon reaches apogee, its position farthest from Earth.

July 24: The Moon enters its final quarter at 8:18 p.m.

July 31: The Black Walnut Leafdrop Moon is new at 11:12 p.m.

The Planets

♃ ♄ ♀ ♂

Moving retrograde into Gemini, Venus is barely visible in the far northwest at sundown early in the month. Late in the month, she appears as the Morning Star in the east just before dawn.

Now in Cancer, Mars continues to hug the western horizon just after dark.

Jupiter in Ophiuchus traverses the southern sky throughout the night, disappearing into the west before sunrise.

Visible in the eastern sky at dusk, Saturn moves with Sagittarius and follows Jupiter along the horizon.

The Stars

In the late evenings of Deep Summer, the teapot-like star formation of Libra lies in the south, followed by Scorpius and its red center, Antares. Sagittarius, the Archer, follows the Scorpion in the southeast. Above the Archer, the Milky Way sweeps up toward Cassiopeia in the north.

In the eastern sky, the stars of the Summer Triangle are moving into position for August. The easiest of these three stars to find is Deneb, which is the large "tail" star of Cygnus the swan (shaped like a large bird in flight, its long neck pointing to the south). To the right of Deneb lies Vega, the brightest star overhead these nights. The third corner of the triangle is Altair, below and about halfway between the other two corners.

The Shooting Stars

The nights of July 28-29 bring the Delta Aquarids after 12:00 a.m. in Aquarius. This shower can bring up to 20 meteors in an hour. The waning crescent Moon should not interfere with your meteor vigil.

Peak Activity Times for Creatures

The following traditional guide to lunar position shows when the Moon is above or below the country, and, therefore, the portion of the day or night during which livestock, people, fish and game are typically the most active and the hungriest.

Activity is likely to increase at New Moon (July 2 and 31) and perigee (July 4) and full Moon (July 15), especially as the barometer falls in advance of cold fronts near those dates.

Ordinarily, the Moon is most powerful when it is overhead (above your position).

Date	Above	Below
July 1:	Mornings	Evenings
July 2 – 8:	Afternoons	Midnight to Dawn
July 9 – 14:	Evenings	Mornings
July 15 – 23:	Midnight to Dawn	Afternoons
July 27 – 31:	Mornings	Evenings

The S.A.D. Stress Index

Seasonal Affective Disorder increases during the hottest days of the year. Many people who suffer from humidity and high temperatures tend to stay indoors like they do in the winter; consequently, they often experience some of the same S.A.D. symptoms they feel in December or January.

An Almanack Horoscope for the Cancer-Leo period of the year offers numerous things with which to practice horoscoping (watching time). Even apartment dwellers can nurture window boxes and indoor plants, good friends to the shut-in who retreats from heat and pollen. African violets under artificial lights in Deep Summer can help bring rooms alive, and those plants remain constant through the year with care. And even in the most threatening heat waves, the Cancer-Leo Sun leaves nights to the stars and planets.

Key for Interpreting the S.A.D. Index:
Totals of 100 to 80: Severe stress
79 to 55: Severe to moderate stress
54 to 40: Moderate stress
39 to 25: Light to moderate stress
24 and below: Light stress

Day	Clouds	Weather	Daylight	Moon	Total
July 2:	5	7	0	15	27
July 4:	5	10	1	18	34
July 15:	4	13	2	25	44
July 21:	2	17	3	2	24
July 24:	1	20	4	5	30

Meteorology
Based on Average Arrival of Weather Systems and the Phases of the Moon

The cool fronts of Deep Summer normally cross the Mississippi River around July 6, 14, 21 and 28. Tornadoes, hurricanes, floods or prolonged periods of soggy pasture are most likely to occur within the weather windows of July 3 through 7, July 18 through 23.

New Moon on July 2 (followed by perigee

on July 4), New Moon on July 31 and full Moon on July 15 may increase the chance of tornadoes in the South and Midwest and the landing of a hurricane in the Gulf region near those dates.

Weekly Weather Estimates
Week 1

Although clouds are relatively rare through the end of June, they often become more frequent on the 1st and 2nd of July. Then, starting on the 3rd, the Sun returns (between showers), and remains through the 11th. Temperatures are generally cooler than those of the previous week. New Moon on the 2nd and perigee on the 7th increase the likelihood of significant rainfall from the Corn Tassel Rains.

Week 2

The Corn Tassel Rains continue through the period, and temperatures, which cooled somewhat during the first days of July, begin to grow warmer. After the 7th, there is a full 90 percent chance that afternoon highs will reach 80 or above. July 7th, 8th and 9th are some of the worst Dog Days of the year: all three bringing a 10 percent chance of heat above 100 degrees.

The period between July 13th and 15th brings cooler conditions in the 70s 25 percent of the years, with the 13th being known to see a high just in the 60s. This July's full Moon on the 15th increases the chances of such cool weather. Nighttime lows typically remain in the 60s, but chilly 50s occur an average of 15 percent of the time.

Week 3

Temperatures are in the 80s and 90s most of the time this week, and, as noted above, highs above 100 are more likely to occur on July 15th and 16th than any other days of the Midwestern year (a 15 percent chance of such heat).

Nighttime lows typically remain in the 60s, but chilly 50s occur an average of ten to 15 percent of the time. Rain is a bit more likely this week than it was last week. Of course, full Moon on the 17th increases the chance of rain and hurricane winds.

Week 4

The coolest days of the week are typically the 22nd and 23rd of the month, when mild 70s are recorded about a fourth of all the years. The 23rd brings pleasant sleeping weather more often than any time in July: a full 35 percent of the nights drop below 60 degrees. The most consistent day of the period, and of the whole month, is the 24th, when highs in the 80s come 95 percent of the time.

Sunshine remains the rule for this week of the month, with three out of four days bringing at least a partial break in the clouds. Chances of rain typically decline as July comes to a close, dropping from 40 to 45 percent on the 24th down to just 20 percent on the 30th and 31st. A cool front passes through the Lower Midwest between the 27th and the 29th, and five years in ten, at least one afternoon in the 70s follows that late-July weather system. Evening lows in the 50s, unusual only two weeks ago, often return. Average high temperatures drop one degree on the 28th, their first decline since late January. New Moon on the 31st increases the likelihood that actual conditions will accelerate that drop this year.

Best Lunar Planting Times

New Moons bookend the month of July, creating two dark-Moon planting periods. During the first in July's first week, seed or set out the major vegetables of the autumn garden: carrots, turnips, beets, collards, kale and broccoli.

In the second dark-Moon period at the end of the month, complete all autumn planting along the 40th Parallel. In northern states along the 45th Parallel, plant spinach for spring and prepare flowers and vegetables for greenhouse culture. Along the 35th Parallel in the South, plant an entire garden; if frost avoids your land this winter, you might bring in a full second or third harvest.

Calendar of Feast Days and Holidays for Farmers, Gardeners and Homesteaders

July 4, 2019: United States (also Puerto Rican)

Independence Day Offer kids and lambs for Independence Day cookouts or tailgate parties at parades and celebrations (take orders).

Almanack Literature
Pliny Fulkner's Amazing Fish Caller

"Dear Poor Will," writes Mrs. Pliny Fulkner from Kentucky, "you will never believe what I am about to tell you, but I swear it is the honest business, no foolin'.

"It all started one night when Pliny and I went out by the water to catch some catfish. And nothing was happening at all. No bites. No tugs on the line. And Pliny was carving on a piece of maple wood that had a funny kind of hole put into it by a bug or something.

"So when Pliny had the wood carved down to maybe about the size of a pencil, he started to chew on one end of it; then he noticed he could blow through the hole in the wood. He started to blow, but you couldn't hear any sound.

"But then the fish started biting. We brought in two nice blues and a big channel cat, but then nothing else. No activity. No fish. An hour later, Pliny started to blow on the carved stick again. Wham! Did we see some action!

"And you can guess what we figured out: that Pliny's piece of wood was a fish caller, and it worked just like a turkey caller or like one of those supersonic bug killing systems.

"And we have tested it and know beyond any doubt it works. Sometimes it takes a while for the caller to produce the desired effect. There are nights we go out to the river and Pliny will blow on that thing for an hour or more before we get a bite. Other times, we get fish right away. Once in a while, we come up with zero, even when other people who don't have a fish caller like Pliny's get their limit, but that's just the way it is with any fish caller.

"Humans can't hear the caller (not even dogs can), and there may be more than one way to blow on it, so Pliny figures it will take him a spell to figure out just how to use it so he'll get the biggest catch."

One of a Kind
By Marlene Arcuri

When I was young, my dad brought home in his pocket this little white beagle with a black eye and a black spot on his side. We called him Jiggs. We tried to teach him to walk on a leash, but any time someone got behind him, he would sit down.

He loved to go hunting. Daddy just had to pick up his gun or hunting coat and Jiggs was ready to go. He liked to hunt on his own, too, and one day he came up missing.

Now there was a little white terrier-type stray dog with a crippled back leg that had adopted us before Jiggs arrived, and he and Jiggs were friends. And after Jiggs disappeared, when we would feed the stray dog, he would take off with his food.

One day after Jiggs had been gone about a

week, Daddy decided to follow the stray dog, and he found out that he was taking his food to Jiggs, who was caught in a groundhog hole out by the railroad tracks.

When Daddy dug Jiggs out, he found that Jiggs had turned himself around in the hole somehow, or maybe he chased the groundhog all the way through. Daddy had to take him to the vet because he had maggots on his back hip. But he lived for a long time. He would sit beside Daddy at mealtime, begging, and it sounded like he was talking to you.

He was a smart little dog.

THE ALMANACK HOROSCOPE
FOR
LEO INTO VIRGO
IN AUGUST
2019

Repetition often removes the distinction between immediate experience and memory. In the case of the seasons, for example, it blurs the line between one summer and the next. All summers become one summer. The observation of one flower during one year merges with those observations in the past and future. The years become one year, reflection and hope indistinguishable. Time loses its power. Change becomes layered, full of connecting radii, consciousness free.

Leon Quel

The Gregorian Calendar

S	M	T	W	T	F	S
				1	2	3
4	5	6	7	8	9	10
11	12	13	14	15	16	17
18	19	20	21	22	23	24
25	26	27	28	29	30	31

Cosmic Children

5:00 a.m. – Gibbous Moon setting behind the locust trees. After a soft, long, night rain, low, round clouds drift from the west, uncovering the moonlight in creases and lumps. High-pitched screech of tree or ground crickets. Katydids low and distant.

I stand in the dark, deaf to the sources of the sounds, aware that I can only hear a fraction of what is happening around me. My references that describe different insect calls help a little, but recordings of this cricket or that cricket mostly demonstrate that my hearing is not good enough to hear them all.

So I can identify maybe three kinds of crickets, and I know that I am only able to hear a fraction of the species that live in my neighborhood. I conclude that I must accept the immensity of my inability and my lack of awareness of all but the tiniest fraction of what is happening.

The first cardinal sings at 6:07 a.m. I ruminate more about the fragments that I perceive, about how incompletion is the normal state of things, how immersed in the world I am, but isolated, too, separated from the outside by my inability to sense all that is holding me in place.

I can only fall back upon random detail to make the world of what I know from rippling, disconnected meteors of sound and color. I write down the number of butterflies in my garden each day. I keep track of bird calls (the ones I can hear). I note the beginning and the end of flower bloom.

If I cannot see every facet of the Great Comet Time itself come back, I can at least watch a few of its shining, cosmic children reappear year after year, comforting, filling in my insufficiency with repetition and maybe even with a promise of understanding.

Steady cardinal calls and high, un-named crickets at 6:30 a.m. Zinnias, orange and violet, red and yellow, slowly take form and color in the twilight by 6:34. Crows wake at 6:40, cardinals quieting down a few minutes later. Then comes the all-day chanting of the sparrows.

The Leo-Virgo Sun

Below Böotes thou seest the Virgin
An ear of corn held sparkling in her hand
Aratos

On August 22, Cross-Quarter Day, the Sun reaches the halfway point between summer solstice and autumn equinox. Leaving behind the stability of Leo, the Sun enters the more volatile sign of Virgo, the first of the most violent periods of change in the second half of the year.

Throughout the last weeks of Leo, high Late Summer still holds sway. Cicadas and katydids and crickets are still boisterous in the night. Fold-wing skippers still chase one another in the morning sunlight. Great colonies of ants migrate. Beds of false boneset and trellises of virgin's bower bloom. Tall blue bellflower and burdock and euonymus keep their blossoms, and fields glow with wingstem, tall coneflowers, early purple ironweed, late bouncing bets and black-eyed Susans.

The latest wildflowers of the year, the heralds of early fall, are set to open. Bur marigolds, zigzag goldenrod, tall goldenrod, Jerusalem artichokes, broad-leafed swamp goldenrod, New England asters and small-flowered asters are budding.

In cooler afternoons, the wind becomes more pungent, sweeter, sharper, maybe from apples down or peach drop, maybe from the woods and undergrowth aging, mellowing as Cross-Quarter Day approaches. When the air is wet and thick, fogs form in the hollows before dawn.

Buckeyes and black walnuts and Osage fruits are heavy on their branches. Green acorns are browning, brittle in their clusters. Joe Pye weed is graying in the wetlands. In the woods, lopseed and panicled tick trefoil are fading, white snakeroot blooming, jumpseeds jumping, touch-me-nots popping, Virginia creeper and sumac reddening sometimes this early.

Skunk cabbage has decayed, and the swamps are littered with its stalks near the purple loosestrife and the great pink water mallow and the American lotus. Most of the sycamore bark has fallen, its shedding near completion for the year. Japanese knotweed is budding. Crab apples have all ripened. Yellow sow thistles line the roads, blue chicory, deep violet ironweed, golden wingstem, silver Queen Anne's lace beside them.

Katydids and crickets begin their chants when cicadas rest at dusk. The katydids often stop their rasping calls hours before sunup; crickets sing until morning twilight. Through the night, only an occasional firefly tells of Deep Summer.

The Black Walnut Leafdrop Moon and the Autumn Apple Picking Moon

One of the earliest trees to shed its leaves is the black walnut. Leo and Virgo often accelerate the walnut's leaf drop, which forecasts the more dramatic foliage collapse of Libra and Scorpio.

The Black Walnut Leafdrop Moon alerts the monarchs and swallowtails and the fall webworms to prepare for autumn. Sparrows form larger flocks. Robins emerge from their Deep Summer retreats.

Great murmurations of starlings become more common. Peaches, plums, grapes, blackberries, second-crop raspberries and elderberries sweeten, then complete their seasons. Yellowjackets come to feed on the fallen fruit.

Catching Late Summer in its great circular web, the giant arabesque orb-weaver spins its first patterns in time with the last generation of wildflowers and the first dusky shadows on the high trees. In the woods, webs of the smaller but more common micrathena spiders often block your walking paths.

The floral markers of Late Summer, the burdock, ragweed, knotweed, boneset, Joe Pye weed, field thistles, coneflowers and oxeye all retreat. Following the spider forecasts, the damp mornings and evenings call toadstools from the lawn and pasture, and fat, white puffball mushrooms from the woods.

Flowers of the arrowhead plant turn to seeds along lake shores, chlorophyll draining from its long stems, leaves paling. The blossoms of the wandering mint above it darken. Early touch-me-not pods explode now when tapped lightly. The fat, bumpy fruits of the Osage orange thump to the ground, their slow decay over the next six months measuring the days to April.

August 2: New on July 31, the Black Walnut

Leafdrop Moon reaches perigee at 2:08 a.m.
New Moon and perigee, so close together and near the average date for the first major cool wave of August, create ideal conditions for turbulent weather.

August 7: The Moon enters its second quarter at 12:31 p.m.
This period between new and full Moon is likely to bring oppressive humidity and heat throughout much of the United States, giving way to storms and cool winds as the Moon turns full.

August 15: The Moon is full at 7:29 a.m.
After full Moon, lunar influence wanes and contributes to a relatively peaceful (but hot and humid (next ten days.

August 17: The Moon reaches apogee at 6:23 a.m.

August 23: The Moon enters its last quarter at 9:56 a.m.

August 30: The Autumn Apple Picking Moon is new at 5:37 a.m. and reaches perigee at 10:57 a.m.
This Moon oversees the last cold front of August and will bring frost to the North and chilly autumnal temperatures to the land along the 40th Parallel.

The Planets

♃ ♄ ♂ ♀

Now in Leo, Venus and Mars accompany bright Arcturus, rising from the east near dawn, moving west throughout the day, lying along the western horizon after sundown. Both planets may be very difficult to see due to their proximity to the Sun.

Still in Ophiuchus, Jupiter is the most reliable evening companion and can be found in the southern sky after dark. Below and a little east of Jupiter, Saturn rides Sagittarius in the center of the southern horizon at dusk and is visible as it moves toward the west throughout the night.

The Stars

Now the Milky Way cradles Cygnus and its greatest star, Deneb, in the east night sky. Below Cygnus, Aquila spreads from Altair. Almost overhead, Vega is the brightest star in Lyra. Due south swims Delphinus, the Dolphin, and in the west, Virgo sets below Böotes and its most prominent star, Arcturus.

When all those clusters are positioned in the sky at midnight, then the Early Summer birds are quiet, ragweed pollen is in the air, blackberries are sweet, hickory nuts and black walnuts are falling, and the foliage of the black walnut trees is coming down. Katydids and cicadas and late crickets are singing.

The Shooting Stars
In the season of late August star-fall,
When the first crickets crinkled the dark...

Robert Penn Warren

The Perseid meteors peak August 12-13 in the east an hour or so after midnight below the Milky Way in Perseus. This shower can produce up to 60 meteors in an hour but the fat Moon is likely to outshine many of them.

***

The Perseids, rising out of winter's Taurus and Orion, cut across Perseus and Andromeda, Cassiopeia and Pegasus, and they pierce an old child-like sense of endless summer when time seemed to last forever, and we were lulled by the lack of experience, or by the lack of familiarity with the seasons and by disbelief that anything so fine as the beauty of August could really disappear.

The Perseid starfall of Late Summer unmasks the fantasy of permanence, and the time watcher might see these meteors as a pivotal sign of autumn's approach. Then it is time to look more closely, become even more aware of the pieces of the world and of the solar events that transform them.

Peak Activity Times for Creatures

The following traditional guide to lunar position shows when the Moon is above or below the country, and, therefore, the portion of the day or night during which livestock, people, fish and game are typically the most active and the hungriest.

Activity is likely to increase at New Moon (August 30) and perigee (August 2) and full Moon (August 15), especially as the barometer falls in advance of cold fronts near those dates.

Ordinarily, the Moon's position overhead (above your location) is more powerful than its position below your location.

Date	Above	Below
August 1 – 6:	Afternoons	Midnight to Dawn
August 7 – 14:	Evenings	Mornings
August 15 – 22:	Midnight to Dawn	Afternoons
August 23 – 29:	Mornings	Evenings
August 30 – 31:	Afternoons	Midnight to Dawn

The Seasonal Affective Disorder Index

In Late Summer, Seasonal Affective Disorder typically depends more on heat and humidity than on the day's length or cloud cover. People who stay indoors to avoid the weather often suffer from a cabin fever not dissimilar to the "winter blahs."

The lengthening of the night can surprise those

who don't pay attention. Then it seems that suddenly the summer is collapsing. Under Gemini and Cancer, so many natural signs of new life were obvious; Leo and Virgo, however, show different signs, and the mind-body of humans makes continual adjustments in order to compensate for the change.

Of course, in the Almanack Horoscope, what you see is what you get. The rich colors and scents and tastes of the Leo-Virgo Sun, and all the events that take place under the Black Walnut Leafdrop Moon easily create a positive balance to this time in nature, only waiting to be observed and embraced.

Day	Clouds	Weather	Daylight	Moon	Total
August 2:	0	20	4	22	46
August 7:	0	10	4	5	19
August 15:	0	15	6	22	46
August 23:	0	15	7	5	27
August 30:	0	11	9	25	45

The Allergy Index
Estimated August Pollen Count

(On a scale of 0 - 700 grains per cubic meter) Most of the pollen in the air this month comes from ragweed.

August 1: 35

August 5: 40

August 10: 50

August 15: 85

August 20: 160

August 25: 200

August 30: 300

Estimated August Mold Count
(On a scale of 0 - 7,000 grains per cubic meter)

August 1: 4000   August 5: 4800
August 10: 6000   August 15: 4000
August 20: 4800   August 25: 5100
August 30: 5500

Meteorology
Based on Average Arrival of Weather Systems and the Phases of the Moon

The cool fronts of Late Summer ordinarily reach the Mississippi River around August 4, 10, 17, 21 and 29. Tornados, hurricanes, floods or prolonged periods of soggy pasture are most likely to occur within the weather windows of August 8 and 15 and between August 27 and 31.

Lunar perigee on August 2 (close to New Moon time on July 31) and the New Moon on August 30 (combined with perigee on the same date), and full Moon on August 15 are likely to strengthen fronts due near those dates.

Weekly Weather Estimates
Week 1

The Dog Days ordinarily continue this week of the year, the daily possibility of highs in the 80s and 90s remaining near July levels. However, August 3, 4, and 5 are the last days of the summer on which there is a 40 percent chance of highs in the 90s, and chances of highs in the 80s are steady at around 50 percent.

Cool days do occur 15 to 25 percent of the years, and afternoons only in the 60s are occasionally recorded between August 2 and 11. (This year, lunar perigee on the 2nd is likely to break the heat at least a little.) Morning lows are typically in the 60s, although one fourth of the nights carry temperatures in the middle 50s. Lunar perigee and New Moon early this week will contribute to pulling the mercury to the 50s or below in many areas above the 40th Parallel.

Week 2

This week's highs: 50 percent of the afternoons are in the 80s, 25 percent in the 90s and another 25 percent in the 70s. Rainfall is typically light, with the 9th, 12th, 13th, and 14th carrying just a 10 to 15 percent chance of a shower. With the arrival of the August 10th cold front, however, the 10th and 11th have a 40 percent chance of precipitation as well as the slight possibility of a high only in the 60s for the first time since July 13th. The 10th through the 14th are likely to bring evening lows below 60 degrees. And within the next seven days, lows reach into the 40s fifteen times more often than they do during the first week of August. Full Moon on the 15th makes 40s much more likely around that date.

Week 3

The weather in the third week of August is somewhat stable, bringing highs in the 90s on 15 to 20 percent of the afternoons, milder 80s 55 percent of the time, and cool 70s the remaining 25 percent. Full Moon on the 17th favors cool 70s! Chances of rain increase from 25 percent at the beginning of the period to 30 percent by August 21st, and then drop abruptly to just 15 percent on the 22nd.

Week 4

This is the week that frost becomes possible in the northern states; snow even occurs at the upper elevations in the Rocky Mountains and in Canada. Here in the Midwest, the third major high pressure system of the month brings chances of highs in the 70s a full 40 percent of the time on August 24, the first time since July 6 that odds have been so good for milder weather.

As that cool front moves east, the period between August 25 and August 27 usually brings a return of warmer temperatures in the 80s or 90s. The 26th, 27th, 28th and 29th each carry a 30 percent chance of highs in the 90s, and the 25th and 26th are the last days of the year on which there is only a ten to 15 percent chance of mild weather in the 70s.

On the 28th, however, the final cool wave of August approaches, and even though chances of 90s remain strong, the likelihood of chilly highs only the 60s or 70s jumps to 30 percent. August 30 is typically the coldest day of the month, and it brings a 50 percent chance of a high just in the 70s, the first time chances of that have been so good since the last day of June.

Nights in the 40s or 50s continue to occur an average of 40 percent of the time, and (thanks to New Moon and perigee) the mornings of the 29th and 30th brings the slight possibility (a 5 percent chance) of light frost, for first time since the beginning of June. Chances of rain are typically 35 percent per day now, with the exception of August 28, on which date thunderstorms cross the region 65 percent of the years in my record.

Best Lunar Planting Times

Seed plants for autumn and winter flowers and vegetables that will produce fruit above the ground near the New Moon (July 31 and August 30). Throughout the South, seed root crops out of doors under the dark last quarter of the Moon (August 23-30).

Calendar of Feast Days and Holidays for Farmers, Gardeners and Homesteaders

August 6, 2019: Jamaican Independence Day
Demand may increase for older lambs, rams or ewes, up to 65 pounds at this time.

August 10, 2019: Ecuadorian Independence Day
Consider reaching out to the Hispanic market at this time to provide lambs and kids for cookouts.

August 12, 2019: Eid al-Adha: (Festival of Sacrifice) Lambs in the range of 55 to 80 pounds are favored for this market.

August 31 – September 28, 2019: Al Hijirah Muharram This celebration of Islamic New Year continues for 29 days. It has no religious significance, but, like many New Year celebrations, it is a cultural event. A rise in halal sales could be expected during this period.

Almanack Literature
Smart Lamb
by Sonia Clements

I am the postmaster in our small town, and one of my route carriers has a small herd of sheep, as I do. One day, he ended up with an extra lamb and asked if I would I take it. I don't ever remember saying yes, but I did end up with the lamb.

As we rode home the 14 miles, she in my passenger seat at least part of the time, I could just tell she was going to get even more spoiled. When we got home, I put her down in the lamb pen, and I went to tend to my second love, flowers. The crying got to me, and I went down and let her out. Of course, she followed me to the house. She had no problem getting up the six steps onto the deck or down the six steps to the back yard with me.

Needless to say, she became part of the family. If you were to open a door to go in the house, she could beat you in it. She would just go in the house and walk around like she owned the place.

Now that you know the history of Lamb, as we called her, you need to know the reasons that I think she is so smart.

She got so that she would come up on the deck, scratch the door to get our attention, then she would step back about four steps so that she could see in the window to see if anyone was coming to the door to open it and come out to see her.

She spent all the time she could on the deck or in the yard with us. When I would leave the house to go on my walk, she and our dog Lacy would have to go with me.

Our favorite thing that she did was that she liked to ride in our six-wheeler. She never even tried to get out or even get too close to the edge. She stood right in the middle with her head right by mine. When I stopped I would tell her to just "stay and I will be right back," and she did. She got kind of heavy to lift in, but she would come running and blatting as soon as she would hear the six-wheeler.

She was also happy to eat the grass and left my flowers alone. That is, until she got a little older. The time that I saw that she had eaten all the flowers off of my trumpet vine planted by my fish pond, AKA Lamb's water tank, I decided that it was time she learned that she IS a sheep, not a human.

It was a rough week or so down at the barn, a few tears, hers and mine, but she got used to it.

When we went down to feed the sheep, she would spend time in the barn with us and, of course, she had her own special dish.

She also learned that in the tack room I kept a large tub with cracked corn and chicken pellets for the ducks at the barn. She decided that it was the best food ever. She would stay in the tack room and eat it while I did the rest of the chores, then she would settle for what was in her dish. When you went down to do chores and did not open the tack room door, soon enough she would go over to the step and stand and scratch the door, letting you know that she needed her special snack.

Lamb has always been special to us, more like a pet than livestock. So that when someone says, "Sheep are so stupid," my husband, Scott, and I have quite a few stories to back up our opinion, and that is that "Sheep are really smart." Lamb is living proof of that.

Tag in the Face
By Ann Witte

Tag was one of those quietly capable Beardies. I had brought him from Scotland as a sire-to-be and working stock dog. He loved working ducks, and from the beginning he was equally gentle with the sheep unless he needed to be tough. I actually had to teach him to bite because he never wanted to use that much force.

One problem I have always had with the sheep must be the basis for that old saw, "The grass is greener on the other side of the fence," because the fool lambs would get their heads stuck reaching through the fence and then bawl. Had any been left trapped in the summer, it would have roasted to death.

Every morning and evening when Tag and I went out, he would stop to listen carefully; and if he heard a stuck lamb, he would insist I help it get free. He would lead me to where that lamb was stuck.

Once I had the lamb firmly trapped between my knees, Tag would go as close to the fence as possible so that the lamb wanted to back out. As I would tuck in the ears and turn the lamb's head, the dog would walk up close to stare in the sheep's face. It would immediately back up more and the head came free. Off would boing the lamb, while Tag would wag his tail "task completed."

Bill Felker

THE ALMANACK HOROSCOPE
FOR VIRGO INTO LIBRA
IN SEPTEMBER
2019

Let sunlight slip from overhead
and slant toward afternoon.
Let evening cool more quickly
than before, and morning warm
more slowly. Let what blooms move
from pink to russet, from lemon to
deepest gold, from baby blue to aster-purple.
Let leaves abandon green for warmer hues.
Let breezes grow cool, rains grow chill,
sleeves grow long. Let thoughts turn
once more toward the woodstove
and second quilts appear on beds.
Let nights grow longer
at the expense of days.
Let autumn come, as it must;
be not afraid. No season has
the final word, but takes its turn.

Deborah Walker, *Let Autumn Come*

The Gregorian Calendar

S	M	T	W	T	F	S
1	2	3	4	5	6	7
8	9	10	11	12	13	14
15	16	17	18	19	20	21
22	23	24	25	26	27	28
29	30					

Reenactment

I am owner of the sphere,
Of the seven stars and the solar year....

Ralph Waldo Emerson

Throughout the woods, tall wood nettle, honewort, waterleaf, wingstem, ironweed, weathering May apples and touch-me-nots have obscured the web of spring, hidden all the trilliums, the violet cress, the ragwort, the purple phlox, toothwort, Jack-in-the pulpit and bluebells.

In my garden, giant hosta leaves have covered the foliage of snowdrops, aconites, crocus and scilla. Pigweed, creeping Charlie, wild violets, waterleaf, dandelions and amaranth have filled in all around the remnants of the April windflowers. The stalks of hyacinths, daffodils and tulips have fallen over and are ceding to the next planting of zinnias and Mexican sunflowers.

A listing of those flowers is like a recitation of historical facts. Like dates or events in human history, they are lost or do not make sense unless they are recreated in my mind. Memory and imagination tell the stories, fill in the setting with details of sound, taste, texture and color and odor, and connect the stories to other stories.

The meaning of natural history, like the meaning of human history, is dependent on my reenactment of what I see happen or of what I believe happened. Without the thinking of or the telling of what has occurred, things lose their place, become disconnected, make no sense. So I go back over what has taken place in the woods and garden. I relive as best I can the steps that brought me here, review their sequences pulled from underneath the overgrowths of previous phases.

The sediment of passage dissolves so quickly. Natural science only goes part of the way. It is I who must move beyond the names and dates, defend imperfect memory and insufficient data with imagination, and fill in the past with my own truth. I am, like Emerson might suggest, "the owner of the sphere," and I am responsible for not only my own narrative but for that of the world around me.

The Virgo-Libra Sun

Autumn equinox occurs (and the Sun enters its Middle Autumn sign of Libra) at 2:50 a.m. on

September 23. Within several days of that moment, the night is about 12 hours long almost everywhere in the continental United States.

Libra straddles the phases of autumn all along the 40th Parallel, ending almost all the wildflower seasons and accompanying the most dramatic phase of leafturn in the entire year. Although Scorpio (October 23 to November 22) shatters the last of the canopy, Libra takes the earlier trees, especially the ashes and locusts, then quickly colors the rest of the maples.

The transition of so many aspects of the natural world from one level of growth to another, the chilling of the nights, the silencing of the birds and the slowing of the crickets, often overturns and fractures perspective.

But when the low Sun is bright in Libra and the woodland canopy is still strong, and buds appear where leaves are absent and next year's spring bulbs grow slowly and steadily beneath the mulch, then a time watcher may see fulfillment more than closure.

The Virgo-Libra Sun sends mixed messages, for sure, and a horoscope in nature reveals the vulnerability of anyone who holds on too tightly to the summer. Nevertheless, if the autumn harvest – spiritual or physical – is less than desired, the Sun offers lessons in adaptation, reevaluation and hunkering down.

The Autumn Apple Picking Moon and the High Leaf Color Moon

At the approach of Libra and equinox, the soybean fields turn yellow and the autumn apple harvest begins under the Autumn Apple Picking Moon. Wood nettle seeds are black when the year's fall apples are the sweetest. Wingstem and ironweed, which overwhelm the woodland paths in August, complete their cycles. Buckeyes pop from their hulls. More hickory nuts and more acorns come down. The huge, pink mallows of the wetlands die back, heads black, leaves disintegrating. Scattered in the pastures, milkweed pods are full, straining, ready to open. Dry mullein stalks stand tall like cacti.

By Full Moon time, puffball mushrooms swell up among spring's rotting stems and leaves. Bees are everywhere in the fields, sometimes five or six on a single flower cluster. Grackles become louder in the afternoons, but an entire morning can go by without a cardinal song or the call of a dove. Wood nettle has gone to seed. Along the freeways, the umbels of Queen Anne's lace, so bright through Deep Summer, are contracting and darkening. Cicadas have begun to die, their brittle bodies appearing all around the yard.

As the Autumn Apple Picking Moon cedes to the High Leaf Color Moon, the first goldenrod goes to seed. White vervain is gray, streaked with maroon, tattered, laced from insects. Boneset is rusting. Beggarticks are ready to stick to your clothing. Roadside sunflowers and Jerusalem artichokes suddenly wither. Black walnut trees are bare. But all across the northern half of the United States, the great time of mapleturn, hickoryturn and oakturn offer brief but brilliant compensation.

September 5: The Autumn Apple Picking Moon enters its second quarter at 10:10 p.m.
New on August 30, this Moon swells crescent in the early days of September, then gibbous as it becomes full, on the 13th.

September 13: The Moon reaches apogee at 8:32 a.m. and becomes full at 11:23 p.m.
The coincidence of full Moon near the September 12 and 15 cold fronts creates the likelihood of frost across the North, hurricanes in the Caribbean and thunderstorms in the South. Apogee, however, will soften the harsher effects of this full Moon.

September 21: The Moon enters its final quarter at 9:41 p.m.
Between September 14 and 25, weak lunar position favors gentle weather and low seasonal stress.

September 27: The Moon reaches perigee at 9:27 p.m.
Perigee, combined with New Moon on the 28th,

strengthen the final cold front of September, making frost almost certain across the North.

September 28: The High Leaf Color Moon is new at 1:26 p.m.

The Planets

♃ ♄ ♂ ♀

Still in Leo, Mars is quite difficult to spot in the east before sunrise or in the west near sundown. Moving once again retrograde, Venus follows Virgo, briefly becoming an Evening Star in the far west near sunset.

As Venus sinks into the western horizon, Jupiter becomes a prominent Evening Star, shining in Ophiuchus in the southwest. Visible at dusk in Sagittarius, Saturn follows Jupiter into the southwest after midnight.

The Shooting Stars
No meteor showers occur this month.

The Stars
The evenings of late Virgo and early Libra bring Perseus rising out of the northeast, the Great Square filling the eastern sky, Cygnus the Swan

overhead, Hercules and the Corona Borealis in the west, and the Big Dipper low in the northwest. Delphinus, the Dolphin, swims across the south. Above it, near the North Star, Cepheus will be situated between Cassiopeia (to the east) and Draco (to the west). Just below the southeastern corner of Cepheus, the star cluster of Lacerta lies in the Milky Way.

Taurus and the Pleiades are up by midnight, and they stay in the dark sky until Middle Spring when their disappearance coincides with the birds' return. Throughout the night, the Milky Way runs from east to west across the sky.

By dawn, the stars of the Summer Triangle are setting in far west, and Orion is climbing up from the eastern horizon. Hercules, which was overhead at 12:00 a.m. in the first week of June, is now setting in the northwest, and Castor and Pollux, the twins of Gemini are peeking over the tree line in the northeast.

Peak Activity Times for Creatures

The following traditional guide to lunar position shows when the Moon is above or below the country, and, therefore, the portion of the day or night during which livestock, people, fish and game are typically the most active and the hungriest.

Activity is likely to increase at New Moon

(September 28) and perigee (September 27) and full Moon (September 13), especially as the barometer falls in advance of cold fronts near those dates.

Ordinarily, the Moon is most powerful when it is overhead (above your position).

Date	Above	Below
September 1 – 4:	Mornings	Evenings
September: 5 – 12:	Afternoons	Midnight to Dawn
September 13 – 21:	Evenings	Mornings
September 21 – 27:	Midnight to Dawn	Afternoons
September 28 – 30:	Mornings	Evenings

The S.A.D. Stress Index

September's relatively pleasant temperatures and clear skies keep Seasonal Affective Disorder at bay throughout most of the month.

Apogee softens the power of the full Moon on September 13, but perigee within a day of New Moon on September 28 doubles the likelihood of lunar-related stress as well as of frost and unstable weather conditions at that time.

Hormonal energy may increase at this time of year, creating an "autumn surge" that combats S.A.D. In addition, numerous signals from fauna and flora (observed and named or not) alert the horoscoper to coming changes in the season. The resulting anticipation at the approach of a landscape entirely transformed in shape and color and sound often reverses any negative effects of the shortening day, frost and the Moon.

Key for Interpreting the S.A.D. Index:
Totals of 100 to 80: Severe stress
79 to 55: Severe to moderate stress
54 to 40: Moderate stress
39 to 25: Light to moderate stress
24 and below: Light stress

Day	Clouds	Weather	Daylight	Moon	Total
September 4:	0	8	9	10	27
September 13:	0	11	10	20	41
September 21:	2	4	12	10	28
September 27:	4	8	13	28	53

Meteorology
Based on Average Arrival of Weather Systems and the Phases of the Moon

Weather history suggests that the cold waves of Early Fall usually cross the Mississippi River on or about the following dates: September 2, 8, 12, 15, 20, 24 and 29.

Tornadoes, hail, floods or prolonged periods of soggy pasture are most likely to occur in connection with tropical storms, near **full Moon on September 13, and at the end of the month with lunar perigee on September 27 and New Moon on September 28, which will coincide with the last cold front of the month.**

Weekly Weather Estimates
Week 1

The effects of the first September cold wave and New Moon on August 30 should appear by the 2nd, which is the first day since June 4th that 90s become unlikely. Then on the 3rd, there is a 55 percent chance of highs only in the 70s, and the chances of frost suddenly become one in a hundred.

The long period during which there is at least a 10 percent chance of highs below 70 degrees begins on September 4th. Warmer conditions typically return on the 5th and 6th, but the second high-pressure system of the month, which arrives between the 5th and 11th, pushes lows into the 30s one year in 20.

September 6 is the first day of the season on which there is about a 5 percent chance of light frost on the gardens of the Lower Midwest. Chances increase at the rate of about 1 percent per day through the 15th of the month. Between the 15th and the 20th, chances grow at the rate of 2 percent per day. Between the 20th and 30th, they grow at the rate of 5 percent per day.

Week 2

Early Fall arrives along the 40th Parallel during the second week of September. Average highs fall below 80, and normal nighttime lows move below 60 until the second week of June. Chances of highs in the 90s hold at less than 10 percent each day this week, the first time that has happened since the end of May. Highs in the cold 60s occur another 10 percent of the time (with the possibility of 50s for the first time since June 4), with 70s and 80s sharing the remaining 80 percent.

The rainiest days this week are historically the 9th and the 12th, each having a 40 percent chance of showers. The other days of the period carry about half those odds. Frost is rare at this stage of September, but chances of a light freeze increase to 10 percent on the 13th and 14th as the third high pressure system of the month arrives in the wake of the full Moon.

Week 3

The third week of September brings one of the most radical autumnal swings so far in the season. Not only do the chances of highs only in the 60s move from 10 percent to 30 percent, but cold afternoons in the 50s also become possible for the first time since June 4.

The likelihood of warm 90s or 80s falls sharply throughout the period, with September 18 bringing only a 20 percent chance of highs above the 70s, the first time that has happened since May 6th. Each day this week brings at least a 30 percent chance of showers, with the 18th having the highest chance: almost 50 percent.

The mornings are chilly, and the possibility of a light freeze grows steadily. Two weeks ago, the odds were high against frost. Now the chance of freezing temperatures in a seven-day period is up to 40 percent. Next week it will be 50 percent. In two more weeks, it will be 80 percent, and in three weeks almost 100 percent.

Week 4

Equinox parallels a drop in extremes as well as in averages. Days in the 90s are rare after the 22nd of September, and even 80s will be gone in about three weeks. The odds for an afternoon in the 50s or 60s this week doubles over those odds last week. The season of light frosts deepens in the Middle Atlantic region; the 24th and the 27th even carry a 20 percent chance of a mild freeze - the greatest chance since May 10th. On the 23rd and the 26th, chances of a high below 70 degrees are better than 50 percent, the first time that has happened since May 4th. New Moon and perigee at September's end will greatly increase the likelihood of cold.

Frostwatch

The following chart shows the chances that frost will have occurred at average elevations along the 40th Parallel by the date indicated. The data can be adjusted by adding 5 percent for each 100 miles north or south of the 40th parallel.

Date	*Chance of Light Frost*	*Chance of Killing Frost*
September 1:	5%	0%
September 10:	10%	1%
September 15:	15%	2%
September 20:	30%	3%
September 25	55%	5%
September 30:	80%	8%

The Allergy Index
Estimated September Pollen Count
(On a scale of 0-700 grains per cubic meter)

September 1: 300
September 5: 240
September 10: 160
September 15: 60
September 20: 10
September 30: 10

Estimated September Mold Count
(On a scale of 0-7,000 grains per cubic meter)

September 1: 5500
September 5: 4800
September 10: 4300
September 15: 2600
September 20: 3600
September 25: 1500
September 30: 1300

Best Lunar Planting Times

Seed plants for autumn and winter flowers and vegetables that will produce fruit above the ground near the new Autumn Apple Picking Moon (August 30 and the High Leaf Color Moon on September 28). Throughout the South, seed root crops out of doors after full Moon (September 13).

Calendar of Feast Days and Holidays for Farmers, Gardeners and Homesteaders

August 31 - September 28, 2019: Al Hijirah/ Muharram This celebration of Islamic New Year continues for 29 days. It has no religious significance, but, like many New Year celebrations, it is a cultural event. A rise in halal sales could be expected during this period.

September 2, 2019: Labor Day

September 10, 2019: Ashura This date commemorates the martyrdom of Muhammad's grandson, Hussein. It also celebrates Noah's survival from the Great Flood.

September 13 - 15, 2019: Harvest Moon Festival or Chuseok Often observed by Korean Americans and others of Asian descent.

September 28 - 30, 2019: Rosh Hashanah Jewish New Year and first High Holiday. Some sub-sects also celebrate the creation of man on this date.

September 29 - October 7, 2019: **Navaratri /Navadurgara** This Hindu feast honors the goddess

Durga. Female animals are typically not used for this celebration.

Almanack Literature
Did the Diet Make the Difference?
By Eugenia Hermann

My family moved to our Indiana farm in 1945. The house was in bad shape, and it took my mother months to get it livable… like layers and layers of sagging wallpaper in almost every room.

Mom's sister had a small grocery in town, and somehow through one of her customers, she located four baby turkeys, and nothing would do but that the turkeys had to come to the farm.

Due to chilly weather, it was decided that the turkeys would be put upstairs in an extra room with a small pen to confine them and a light bulb for heat. Layers of newspaper were used to cover the floor.

All went well until my aunt brought leftover cottage cheese and onion tops from the store. She intended for the turkeys to eat the mixture. Talk about a guzzling, stinking mess! But the turkeys thrived on that particular diet.

Once outdoors, the turkeys grew into huge birds, learning to fly and occasionally even roosting on the house. Then they became like a pack of guard dogs, and I was their prey!

I would make it from the house to the school bus in the morning in relative safety, but getting off the bus in the afternoon and across our large yard was a screaming, hysterical challenge for a first-grader on the run from four angry turkeys.

Needless to say, I was really grateful for Thanksgiving that year, and to this day I wonder how much influence that cottage cheese/onion top diet had on those turkeys' hateful personalities.

Bring the Hoe!
by Sylvia P. Gibbons

This particular experience sounds far-fetched, I know, but it is true...I was there.

I remember when I was seven or eight years old, my parents bought the farm where I still live. The family that owned the farm before us raised hogs, and in the near pasture was a small deserted hog house.

My mom raised turkeys, so one of the hens "moved into" the hog house to hatch her eggs and raise her family. Mom would go over to the old building every two or three days to feed and water the hen. As time came close to hatching date, Mom would gently lift the hen off her nest and sprinkle the eggs with warm water to soften the shells for easier hatching.

One day near the time of hatching, Mom was performing this deed, and we heard her yell. Now we were some distance from the hog house, but we heard her yell quite clearly: "Bring the hoe!"

My dad and two older brothers ran to help, and in the nest, under the turkey, was a big black snake. My dad took the hoe and cut off the snake's head, and inside the snake were all 21 turkey eggs.

Then my brother held the snake's tail while Dad gently squeezed the eggs out of the snake's body. The snake had swallowed all of the eggs, but had not broken any of them.

The turkey hen seemed to take all of this in stride, and, believe it or not, every egg hatched.

THE ALMANACK HOROSCOPE FOR LIBRA INTO SCORPIO IN OCTOBER 2019

A springful of larks in a rolling
Cloud and the roadside bushes brimming with
whistling
Blackbirds and the Sun of October
Summery
On the hill's shoulder,
Here were fond climates and sweet singers suddenly
Come in the morning where I wandered and
listened
To the rain wringing
Wind blow cold
In the wood faraway under me.

Dylan Thomas

The Gregorian Calendar

S	M	T	W	T	F	S
		1	2	3	4	5
6	7	8	9	10	11	12
13	14	15	16	17	18	19
20	21	22	23	24	25	26
27	28	29	30	31		

Virtues and Self-Sufficiency

I grew up surrounded by the power of my mother's prayers and the reserved dedication of my father. My mother's faith, the family knows, interceded with the Virgin to bring my sister safely through rheumatic fever and to protect my father during World War II. Her novenas and her love still shape what happens in my life.

My father promoted a mix of pragmatism and Catholic values, attended mass daily, never seemed an intimate man, but gave me everything he could. I recognize in myself his preparations for the seasons, his need for order, for naming, for setting things in a theological basket.

Virtues are associated with images in my memories. My mother was ironing clothes one afternoon, and I asked her about happiness. She said there were no guarantees; that's why a person prayed.

I remember my father walking with me across the fields in winter, hunting rabbits in the Wisconsin snow. I thought about him in the snows of this past winter, redefining myself and what he meant to me.

He had had his fill of weapons in the South Pacific and wasn't fond of shooting, but he took me out when I was still too young to go by myself, and he tried to guide and tame my first passions for guns. He did it well, and I came from his lessons with respect for life and some skill with a rifle and pistol.

He also once told me never to assume that anyone else was more correct than I might be. I've forgotten the circumstances of his statement; they were probably reasonable; my father was no radical questioner of authority. But he never wanted me to suppose that someone else knew more or better, unless I had good reason.

He would most likely have preferred I remember some different piece of advice, but I remember that one almost above all. It gave me confidence and set me free to question him and to go my own way.

That freedom and the love and the invisible powers of my mother have stood by me, forming the center of my self-reliance and security, smoothing the imperfections in our relationships, and making the foundation for my own adult life.

The Libra-Scorpio Sun

The landscape contains a thousand dials which indicate the natural divisions of time....
Henry David Thoreau

The Sun's passage from Libra to Scorpio on Cross-Quarter Day October 23 tilts the hinge of Middle Autumn and initiates the most dramatic period of leaf fall. Throughout this final stage of the natural year, the landscape becomes fully primed for the new signs and seasons to come.

As the days shorten, the effects of the weakening Sun are easily seen in the collapse of almost all the foliage. Smaller changes also offer measure of Scorpio. The low trills of the field crickets become slow, then rare. Goldenrod flowers darken and turn to downy tufts. Pokeweed berries shrivel and fall. Wingstem turns brittle from the cold. Knotweed withers. Jerusalem artichokes yellow, stalks collapsing.

The last flocks of robins, blackbirds and herring gulls complete their migration. The last sandhill cranes depart their northern nesting grounds, the first formations reaching the Ohio Valley just days before Sagittarius.

The last monarchs sail over the last roses. The last black walnuts and Osage fall. The last raspberry bushes and apple trees give up their fruit. The last autumn violets and dandelions go into dormancy. The last witch hazel blossoms curl in the hard frost.

Milkweed and white snakeroot seeds scatter. Bittersweet opens. Asian lady beetles take shelter in bark and siding. Deer mate in the night. Wings of the hosta droop and melt. Black privet berries and rose hips appear as their foliage thins. Winter wheat sprouts and greens the fields. Skunk cabbage spears push out from the muck, forecasting spring.

As distant and unimaginable as the movements of the firmament seem, so close and tangible and countable are the events of the immediate landscape. Starlike, those events gleam in their Earthly setting, pointing to the hour, the constellations of lanky, empty branches following and reflecting in mirror the high astrology of the sky.

The High Leaf Color Moon and the Sleeping Frog Moon

At the close of Late Summer, the year begins its ascent to the barometric highs of December. By the beginning of October, the waves of barometric pressure that reflect the weather are stronger; the peaks become taller; the lows are deeper, with almost every valley bringing rain or flurries.

The tapering of floral sequences and the gradual surge of leafturn occur amid the remnants of Early Fall. From the broad lowland of warmth with its six months of birdsong and its hundred days of insect calls, the Sun pulls the land up into the foothills of the year where asters and goldenrod bloom and where trees are gold and red.

As the High Leaf Color Moon waxes and wanes throughout the month, the chemical changes in the foliage that became noticeable six weeks ago now accelerate until the fragile landscape turns all at once.

Black walnuts, locusts, buckeyes, box elders, hackberries, ashes and cottonwoods are almost bare, but shagbark hickories, sweet gums, oaks, sassafras and sycamores reach their finest colors.

When the most intense leaf color appears in the maples, then yellow jackets swarm on the windfall apples, New England asters reach the end of their blooming cycle and wild asparagus yellows by the roadsides.

When maple color peaks, then the day has lost about four hours from its summer length, and light snow occurs one year in a decade along the 40th Parallel. Orange bittersweet opens, all its foliage fallen, and the first of last year's Christmas cactus flowers in a south window.

And when the High Leaf Color Moon becomes the Sleeping Frog Moon at the end of the month, light morning frosts become more frequent, and long flocks of blackbirds cross the sky, their passage sometimes lasting five minutes. Winter starlings cackle and whistle in the trees.

In the woodlands quickweed still provides a deep green border to the paths. A few lance-leaf and zigzag goldenrod still hold. A few swallowtails and fritillaries visit the garden. Asters are still common, with chicory and scattered Queen Anne's lace. And in the swamps, skunk cabbage can be two inches high, waiting for February.

October 4: The High Leaf Color Moon enters its second quarter at 11:47 a.m.
The relatively weak position of the Moon during the first ten days of October augurs well for mild conditions.

October 10: The Moon reaches apogee at 1:29 p.m.

October 13: The Moon is full at 4:08 p.m.
The arrival of the mid-October high-pressure system usually puts an end to the mildest time of Early and Middle Fall, and this year, the Full High Leaf Color Moon will definitely intensify the cold.

October 21: The Moon enters its final quarter at 7:38 a.m.
As the Moon wanes after the 13th, conditions improve for a return of gentler weather throughout the northern half of the United States, favoring the development of the best leaf coloring of the year – as well as the nicest weather for traveling to see the leaves.

October 26: The Moon reaches perigee at 5:41 a.m.
Lunar perigee and New Moon at the end of the month will most likely bring precipitation and then frost all across the North. Conditions will be favorable for a hurricane in the Caribbean.

October 27: The Sleeping Frog Moon is new 10:38 p.m.

The Planets

♃ ♄ ♂ ♀

Passing retrograde into Libra, Venus rises too late and sets too early to be easily seen this month. And Mars, in Virgo, will also be difficult to find for the same reasons. Briefly visible in the southwest after Sunset, Saturn quickly sinks into the far west with Sagittarius.

On the other hand, Jupiter remains the great Evening Star, easily seen when it shines in Ophiuchus in the far west after dark.

The Stars

Evenings of late Libra bring the Northern Cross setting in the west, accompanied by Aquila and Lyra. Above you the Great Square lies below the Milky Way. In the east, winter's Orion rises behind Taurus and the Pleiades. In the northern sky, the Big Dipper hugs the horizon. Deep in the southwest, Fomalhaut hovers above the tree line.

An hour or so before sunrise, all the winter constellations will be in place, Orion due south, brilliant Sirius and Procyon in the southeast. In the south-southwest, red Aldebaran and the Pleiades will be following the Great Square. There will also be a promise of warmth: Regulus, the bright planting star of Middle Spring , will be rising ahead of the Sun.

The Shooting Stars

The Draconid meteors fall at the rate of about ten per hour from the constellation Draco to the northwest of the North Star after midnight between October 6 and 10. The crescent Moon is not likely to obscure these shooting stars.

The Orionid meteors appear in Orion in the night of October 21 and 22 at the rate of 15 to 30 per hour. The waning gibbous Moon may obscure some of those meteors with its light.

Peak Activity Times for Creatures

The following traditional guide to lunar position shows when the Moon is above or below the country, and, therefore, the portion of the day or night during which livestock, people, fish and game are typically the most active and the hungriest.

Activity is likely to increase at New Moon (October 27) and perigee (October 26) and full Moon (October 13), especially as the barometer falls in advance of cold fronts near those dates.

Ordinarily, the Moon is most powerful when it is overhead (above your position).

Date	Above	Below
October: 1 – 4:	Afternoons	Midnight to Dawn
October 5 – 12:	Evenings	Mornings
October 13 – 20:	Midnight to Dawn	Afternoons
October 21– 26:	Mornings	Evenings
October: 27 –31:	Afternoons	Midnight to Dawn

The S.A.D. Stress Index
Forces related to Seasonal Affective Disorder

become more apparent in October as the length of the night increases and chances of mild weather decrease. Although cloud cover is ordinarily not a major factor in S.A.D. during the transition time of Libra and Scorpio, the odds for completely overcast conditions rise steadily. Full Moon on the 13th could stress gardeners, and perigee on the 26th, close to New Moon on the 27th, is expected to disrupt moods as well as the weather.

As the forces that tend to increase S.A.D. gather momentum, however, other forces may help to decrease the effect of October's changes. The landscape, so suddenly transformed, can create exhilaration as well as shock and dismay. Often a resurgence in the undergrowth creates the impression of a second spring and a promise of new life in the new year.

The migration of birds may cause a restlessness in humans, a desire to move on in space and time; and while such feelings can be discouraging to those who feel trapped in their situations, they can also reawaken old dreams and strategies for achieving them or for finding compensation for not achieving them. And so the turbulence of Middle Fall not only produces loss but also offers physiological as well as spiritual resources for renewal. In a sense, the higher the S.A.D. Index climbs, the more resources appear in nature.

Key for Interpreting the S.A.D. Index:
Totals of 100 to 80: Severe stress
79 to 55: Severe to moderate stress
54 to 40: Moderate stress

39 to 25: Light to moderate stress
24 and below: Light stress

Day	Clouds	Weather	Day	Moon	Totals
October 4:	5	12	14	10	41
October 10:	6	14	15	8	43
October 13:	7	14	17	22	60
October 21:	9	15	19	10	53
October 26:	11	17	20	25	73

Meteorology
Based on Average Arrival of Weather Systems and the Phases of the Moon

Weather history suggests that the cold waves of Middle Fall are likely to cross the Mississippi River on or about October 2, 7, 13, 17, 23 and 30.

Full Moon on October 13 is likely to intensify the weather system due on that date, and lunar perigee on the 26th and New Moon on the 27th are likely to bring frost to the upper United States as well as the increased likelihood of hurricane formation in the Atlantic.

Weekly Weather Estimates
Week 1
Light frost strikes 10 to 20 percent of all the

nights this week, with October 3rd most likely to bring a damaging freeze in the 20s (a 5 percent chance of that). Highs in the 80s occur on approximately 10 percent of the days, and 70s can be expected 30 percent of the time. Moderate 60s dominate 50 percent of the afternoons, while colder 40s and 50s come 15 to 20 percent of the time.

The likelihood of colder weather almost always increases after the 4th when the chances of highs only in the 50s swells from an average of 15 percent to 30 percent. Rain falls about one day in three. The driest days are the 3rd, the 6th and the 7th, and the wettest days are October 1st and the 4th. Skies are clear to partly cloudy 70 percent of the time. The sunniest days are typically the 3rd and the 6th, when clouds are almost completely absent 80 percent of the time.

Week 2

While some days this week are often warm (the 8th of October bringing a 40 percent chance of highs above 70 degrees), others are typically cooler. October 11, 12 and 13 are the days most likely to see highs in the 40s or 50s. The coldest morning so far in the season usually comes on October 13, when the chances of a low in the 20s are 20 percent for the first time since spring. Full Moon on the 13th, of course, increases those chances.

The first part of the week is usually dry (with only a 20 percent chance of precipitation on the 8th), but precipitation often increases thereafter, with the 10th bringing a 40 percent chance of rain, and the 12th a 50 percent chance. The 12th is also the first day in my weather history that snow has a five to 10 percent chance of falling, and the full Moon will make snow all the more likely.

Week 3

While most afternoons are in the 50s and 60s, the weather does warm up sometimes: the 15th and 16th each have a 35 percent chance of highs in the 70s or 80s, and the other days at least have a 25 percent chance of such temperatures.

Lows in the 20s or 30s are most likely to occur on the mornings of the 19th and 20th, with the latter date carrying the highest chances of a freeze so far this season: a full 30 percent chance of a light frost, and an additional 20 percent chance of a hard freeze.

Most days this week have a 30 percent chance of precipitation, with the 16th and 17th being the wettest (with a 40 percent chance). The times most likely to produce snow are the 18th through the 20th (but only 5 to 10 percent of all the years).

Week 4

Highs are usually in the 50s or 60s, with the odds for 70s near one in five. The danger of frost remains similar to that of the third week in October; about one night in three receives temperatures in the upper 20s or lower 30s. But by this late in the season, the chances of a hard freeze have risen past 50 percent, and the odds get better each night for killing lows. Perigee on the 26th and New Moon on the 27th increase the likelihood of a hard freeze in the North this week and light freeze down into the

Border States.

This week is generally a brighter one than last week. Chances of Sun are about 70 percent throughout the period, and some of the driest October days are the 26th, 28th, and 29th (each having just a 15 percent chance of precipitation).

Frostwatch

The following chart shows the chances that frost will often have occurred by the date indicated. Calculations are based on typical frequency of freezing temperatures at average elevations along the 40th Parallel during the month of October. The data can be adjusted roughly by adding 5 percent for each 100 miles north or south of that Parallel. Local frost histories, of course, offer much greater detail.

Date	Light Frost	Killing Frost
October 1:	80 percent	10 percent
October 5:	85 percent	15 percent
October 10:	90 percent	20 percent
October 15:	95 percent	30 percent
October 20:	98 percent	40 percent
October 25:	100 percent	50 percent
October 30:		75 percent

Best Lunar Planting Times

Late Fall and Early Winter are prime periods for seeding flowers under lights. Sow your seeds as the

Sleeping Frog Moon becomes the New Moon (October 27). Also set in your amaryllis and paperwhite bulbs around this time for holiday blossoms.

Plant the spring garden throughout the South, root crops under the dark last half of the High Leaf Color Moon (October 13-25), crops that produce their fruit above the ground in the first half of the High Leaf Color Moon (October 1-12) and the first days of the Silent Cricket Moon (November 26-30).

Calendar of Feast Days and Holidays for Farmers, Gardeners and Homesteaders

September 29 – October 7, 2019: Navaratri /Navadurgara This Hindu feast honors the goddess Durga. Female animals are typically not used for this celebration.

Almanack Literature
Granny in the Hole!
by Susan Perkins

My now-deceased grandmother owned 80 acres of an island in the Missouri River in the '50s.

Her two sons and two daughters, along with their families, spent many wonderful times there, in the little clubhouse on stilts.

The first spring, the women of the family drew the short straw and had to dig the outhouse hole. The men were to chop weeds in the fencerow and front yard.

The women were busy digging and sweating when they heard laughter coming from the kitchen. There, in plain view, sat the men, drinking beer at the kitchen table.

It was unseasonably hot, and my mom and grannies hatched a plan for one of them to have a stroke and fall in the hole, teaching the men a lesson. It was decided Granny would be the one to take the fall.

She lowered herself into the hole, stretched out as dramatically as possible, while my Mom and Aunt Betty screamed at the top of their lungs, "Your mom's had a stroke! Your mom's had a stroke!"

The men's feet never touched the steps as they jumped from the back porch running.

They gently lifted Granny from the hole, but Granny was losing her game face and starting to grin. My mom pulled her straw hat over her face, but it was too late: her shoulders were beginning to shake with laughter, giving the whole joke away.

The men were so mad that they threw Granny back in the hole and locked the women out of the clubhouse for the rest of the afternoon.

Singing Worms

The last week of September is traditionally Singing Worm Week throughout the nation. As the ground cools, earthworms become more active and begin to use their beautiful voices. Some readers (who wish to remain anonymous for obvious reasons) have even written poems to celebrate this occasion.

In order to appreciate these verses, one vocabulary note may be helpful. An "annelid" is a member of a large class of segmented worms. There, so now you're ready. Here's the first poem, which explores the multifaceted dimensions of worm melodies:

It is quiet, it is hid:
The singing of the annelid.
Some are sweet, some are bittah:
Choruses of annelidah.

People are often surprised at night by singing worms. The following verse tells about such an experience:

All through the night, the sounds did swell
Like teeny voices from heav'n or hell.
I crept up to the garden wall
And peered inside, my ears a-ringing:
Oh my! I saw 'twas WORMS a singing!

In addition to being good singers, worms are quite smart. The worm's analytic ability is celebrated in the following pun-verse:

Now let's salute the thinking worm:
His annelidics make me squirm!

And Jean Nonnamaker is the unabashed author of the following.

Singing Fishworms

In their holes worms must sing
It must have a certain ring.
A robin stands and cocks its head
Waiting to be instantly fed.
The worms' singing gives them away,
Ending what started out a perfect day!!!

THE ALMANACK HOROSCOPE FOR SCORPIO INTO SAGITTARIUS IN NOVEMBER 2019

When after climbing the little winding lane up the hillside, I came out onto the open at the top, I could hardly realize how good it was to be out in the woods again, after months of denial. A dead weed, virgin's bower seeds with a little puff of snow on each cluster, how beautiful. I looked up into the vast gray sky, which was luminous with invisible sunlight behind the clouds, and felt: I am home again - this is mine.

Charles Burchfield

The Gregorian Calendar

S	M	T	W	T	F	S
					1	2
3	4	5	6	7	8	9
10	11	12	13	14	15	16
17	18	19	20	21	22	23
24	25	26	27	28	29	30

Attachment and Befriending

On a recent trip to see the last trees of Late Fall, I paid attention to the way I missed home and summer, and I thought about what caused the discomfort at leaving both behind.

Since my wife died six years ago, I have tried to understand how to come to terms with home. I have become overly attached to the place where I live and to my story contained in its rooms and gardens. It is hard for me to go away.

On the other hand, once I am on the road and look closely at the different landscape, I like the freedom and take comfort in what I find. I do not become detached so much as I befriend the new space and time.

Spring and summer have always been my favorite seasons, and I miss them now. But when I am too sad to see the leaves come down or too fearful of abandoning the safety of my yard, the grip is too strong.

Homesickness comes from holding on and from being held too much. Befriending is an open acceptance of what appears on the other side of home. Each pole is a mentor. Each year, I learn from autumn and the road not to hold summer and home too close and to make friends with the cold and absence.

The Scorpio-Sagittarius Sun

*Our golden Sun is fleeing into Sagittarius,
Leaving days of snow and nights of ice.*

Manuscript of Benedictbeurn,
"De ramis cadunt folia"

Daylight Saving Time ends at 2:00 a.m. on Sunday, November 3. Set clocks back one hour at 2:00 a.m.

On November 23, the Sun leaves the Late Fall sign of Scorpio and enters the Early Winter sign of Sagittarius, three fourths of its way from autumn equinox to winter solstice. At the end of November, Sunset has reached to within just a few minutes of its earliest time throughout the nation. The latest Sunrise, however, is still about half an hour away.

When the Sun came into Sagittarius, the ancient Chinese announced "Stuffing Up Windows Time" or "Turning Jackets Time" in order to signal the advent of the coldest period of the year. Far to the west of Beijing, the 23rd of November was celebrated as St. Clement's Day, the traditional beginning of European winter during the Middle Ages. English children would go "clementing" in that era, sometimes singing verses like the following:

St Clement's, St Clement's comes once in a year
Apples and pears are very good cheer
Got no apples, money will do
Please to give us one of the two.

In the United States centuries later, trick-or-treating takes place a few weeks earlier than clementing used to occur, but the first major shift toward winter still happens early in Sagittarius, accentuated on calendars by Thanksgiving.

The cutting of corn and soybeans is almost always complete by now throughout the nation. Ewes and does have been bred to have their lambs in time for Easter. Pastures stop growing when the ground dips below 50 degrees, but winter wheat, having sprouted under the High Leaf Color Moon, turns the planted landscape emerald green.

Bluebirds make their final passage south as the Sun comes into the sign of Sagittarius. Nourished by the great stands of honeysuckle, robins linger to feed. Starlings whistle and wrens chatter at sunrise. Sparrow hawks become more common as November deepens. Finches work the sweet gum tree fruits, digging out the seeds from their hollows. Humans "stuff their windows" with plastic or modern thermal glass; they bring out their winter coats; they celebrate the harvest.

The Sleeping Frog Moon and the Silent Cricket Moon

Throughout Middle and Late Fall, frogs and toads seek shelter from the coming cold, migrating to protective places underground, in water or in cracks and crevices that will keep them from the forces of Early, Deep and Late Winter

Under the Sleeping Frog Moon, Christmas cacti bud in sunny windows. People plant paperwhite and amaryllis bulbs for the holiday season ahead. As toads and frogs migrate, chickweed grows back all along the woodland paths, and cress revives in pools and streams.

The last crickets still sing in the warmer evenings of the Sleeping Frog Moon, and the last daddy longlegs huddle together in the woodpile. Mosquitoes still wait for prey near backwaters and puddles. Asian lady beetles look for openings in your siding in which to spend the winter. Late woolly bear caterpillars still emerge in the Sun. Cabbage butterflies still look for cabbage. Yellowjackets sometimes come out to look for fallen fruit.

Sandhill cranes start their migration south under the Sleeping Frog Moon, and vast flocks of crows gather to feed and talk.

Then with the advent of the Silent Cricket Moon, especially above the 40th Parallel, the final leaves come down throughout most of the nation, average nighttime temperatures fall below freezing. Under great quilts of snow and fallen fruits and foliage, the frogs and toads fall fast asleep, and the last crickets grow silent.

Let sleeping frogs lie.
Pliny Fulkner

November 5: The Sleeping Frog Moon enters its second quarter at 5:23 a.m.
Lunar position is expected to keep the first week of November relatively mild, extending the post-Halloween period of benign temperatures until full Moon time approaches.

November 7: The Moon reaches apogee (its position farthest from Earth) at 3:37 a.m.
As the Moon moves closer to Earth and waxes gibbous in the days ahead, expect chillier and more turbulent weather.

November 12: The Moon is full at 8:34 a.m.
As has occurred throughout the year, the full Moon will strengthen the mid-November cold fronts.

November 19: The Moon enters its final quarter at 4:11 p.m.

November 23: The Moon reaches perigee (its position closest to Earth) at 2:54 a.m.
Perigee is likely to deepen the power of the November 24 weather system, increasing odds for cold and precipitation.

November 26: The Silent Cricket Moon is new at 10:06 a.m.
New Moon, so close to perigee, will keep the nation in overcoats and will complicate Thanksgiving travel.

The Planets

♃ ♄ ♂ ♀

Remaining in Virgo, Mars continues to rise in the east well before the Sun comes up and is the red Morning Star.

Travelling with Ophiuchus, Venus and Jupiter rise near dawn and move across the sky during the day, visible in some locations in the far west near sundown.

Very low in the southwest in the early evening, Saturn disappears in the middle of the night.

The Stars

Before midnight, early in the month, the Milky Way runs from east to west, cutting the sky in half. Cassiopeia is now due south of Polaris. The Big Dipper hugs the northern horizon, its pointers lying northeast-southwest.

Outriders of winter, the Pleiades move almost overhead, leading on the Hyades and the red eye of Taurus, Aldebaran. Orion towers in the southeast, followed by Sirius and Procyon. Castor and Pollux, the rulers of January, stand above the dogs of Orion. August's Vega is setting now. Cygnus, the swan of the Northern Cross, and the gauge of Late Autumn's progress, is disappearing south.

The Shooting Stars

The South Taurid shower brings a handful of meteors per hour on the evenings of November 5 and 6, and the Moon should not interfere with meteor watching.

The North Taurid Meteors appear on the night of November 12, but the full Moon will brighten the sky on that date, making it much more difficult to find these shooting stars.

The Leonids (at the rate of about 15 per hour) will arrive near the constellation Leo in the eastern sky near midnight on November 18. The waning, rising gibbous Moon may obscure many of these shooting stars.

Peak Activity Times for Creatures

The following traditional guide to lunar position shows when the Moon is above or below the country, and, therefore, the portion of the day or night during which livestock, people, fish and game are typically the most active and the hungriest.

Activity is likely to increase at New Moon (November 26) and perigee (November 23) and full Moon (November 12), especially as the barometer falls in advance of cold fronts near those dates.

Ordinarily, the Moon is most powerful when it is overhead (above your position).

Date	Above	Below
November: 1–2:	Afternoons	Midnight to Dawn
November 3 – 11:	Evenings	Mornings
November 12 – 18:	Midnight to Dawn	Afternoons
November 19 – 25:	Mornings	Evenings
November 26 – 30:	Afternoons	Midnight to Dawn

The S.A.D. Stress Index

The average length of November's night is almost as great as the night's length in December and January; the weather becomes more severe, and clouds thicken. S.A.D. increases to winter levels and the effect of lunar phase and position becomes even more significant.

The year's progress in Scorpio and early Sagittarius, however, does not necessarily produce the meteorological and physiological effects related to S.A.D. Fortunately, attitude and activity may counter clouds, the long nights and cold weather.

The *Almanack* horoscope suggests that the many seasons in the landscape of this time of year offer contrast and cheer to the darkening days.

Early November marks the center of the Season of Second Spring: sweet Cicely, Virginia creeper, burdock, red clover, waterleaf, ground ivy, celandine, sweet rocket, dock and leafcup often revive and look ahead six months to Middle Spring.

Deer Mating Season coincides with Witch Hazel Blooming Season, and the Season of Red Berries throughout the parks as dogwoods, hawthorns, bayberry and flowering crabs reveal their color.

In the greenhouse, Jade Tree Flowering Season and Aloe flowering season complement the gathering tide of Christmas Cactus Flowering Season. Along the West Coast, the annual Crab Harvest Season parallels early Poinsettia Season in the Midwest as Crawdad Season starts in Louisiana, with crawdads moving into flooded rice fields to feed on the remnants of that crop.

The more seasons of Scorpio and Sagittarius you follow, the greater your defenses against the next month's Early Winter, and the easier it may be to hunker down by the fire, away from S.A.D, to enjoy the hermitage of late Sagittarius, Capricorn and Aquarius.

Key for Interpreting the S.A.D. Index:
Totals of 100 to 80: Severe stress

79 to 55: Severe to moderate stress
54 to 40: Moderate stress
39 to 25: Light to moderate stress
24 and below: Light stress

Day	Clouds	Weather	Day	Moon	Totals
November 1:	13	17	22	0	52
November 7:	14	18	23	20	75
November 14:	16	19	23	0	58
November 23:	17	20	24	25	86
November 26:	18	21	24	20	83
November 29:	20	21	25	10	76

Meteorology
Based on Average Arrival of Weather Systems and the Phases of the Moon

Weather history suggests that the cold waves of Late Fall usually cross the Mississippi River on or about November 2, 6, 11, 16, 20, 24 and 28. Snow or rain often occurs prior to the passage of each major front.

If strong storms occur this month, weather patterns suggest that they will happen during the following periods: November 2-5, 14-16 and November 22-27.

It is probable that full Moon on November 12, lunar perigee on November 23 and the New

Moon on November 26, will bring stronger-than-average storms to the United States, complicating Thanksgiving travel.

Weekly Weather Estimates
Week 1

The chances of warmth in the 70s drop to just 5 percent on November 4, and odds increase for cold throughout the week ahead. Highs of just in the 30s or 40s are relatively rare during the final days of October, but by the 5th of November, they occur 25 percent of the time, and chances rise to over 40 percent by the 10th of the month.

The coolest days in this period are typically the 6th and the 7th, both of which have only about a 15 percent chance of warmth in the 60s. The 3rd ushers in the snow season for this part of the country, flurries or accumulation emerging into the realm of possibility, at least a 10 percent possibility per day between that date and spring.

Chances of a thunderstorm virtually disappear until February, but all-day rains increase. The first ten days of November are about twice as rainy as the final ten of October. Chances of rain or snow run at about 40 percent from the 1st through the 5th, then drop to just 15 to 20 percent on the 6th, 7th and 8th.

Week 2

Late Fall almost always arrives by this second week of November. It is a transition season during which the last leaves fall, skies darken, wind speed increases, hard frosts put an end to the year's flower and vegetable cycles, and farmers complete harvest.

High-pressure systems, preceded by clouds and rain or snow, typically cross the Mississippi River around the 9th and the 14th. The 9th is historically the wettest day of November's second week. The 13th is the driest. One partly cloudy afternoon in the 60s or 70s comes six years out of ten during this time of the year, but cold and precipitation are the norm. Full Moon on the 12th will ensure the cold, and double the likelihood of snow or rain on the 10th and 11th.

Week 3

The 15th, 19th and 20th are the days this week most likely to be mild with highs in the 60s. The fifth cold front of the month comes through at the end of the period, and the 21st brings a slight possibility for a high only in the 20s. The 15th is the day most likely to bring precipitation, having a 60 percent chance of rain or snow. The 20th is also fairly damp, carrying a 50 percent chance. The 18th is the driest day of the week; it has only a 20 percent chance of showers or flurries.

Week 4

The third week of Late Fall, is typically a stark and windy week that marks the decline of average highs below 50 degrees throughout the region, and the end to any reasonable chance of a day above 70. Nights below zero even become possible now. The sixth cold front of the month, arriving around the 24th, often brings rain on the 23rd (there is a 50 percent chance of that with lunar perigee occurring on that day). The seventh high-pressure system generally arrives on November 28, preceded by rain 70 percent of the time on the 27th, that date being the wettest day in the month's weather history. November 28th, 29th and 30th have the best odds of the month for snow. After the 25th, the percentage of cloudy days almost doubles over the average for the rest of November, and the New Moon on the 26th should increase the odds for a stormy end to the month.

Best Lunar Planting Times

This month is one of the best of all for seeding bedding plants for spring flowers. Sow your seeds under lights near the new Sleeping Frog Moon, (October 27) and the new Silent Cricket Moon (November 26). Holiday bulbs like paperwhites and amaryllises are more likely to flower near Christmas if planted at the end of October.

Plant the spring garden throughout the South, root crops under the dark last half of the Sleeping Frog Moon (November 13-25), crops that produce their fruit above the ground in the first half of the Sleeping Frog Moon (November 1-11) and the first days of the Silent Cricket Moon (November 26-30).

Calendar of Feast Days and Holidays for Farmers, Gardeners and Homesteaders

November 10, 2019: Muhammad's Birthday (Mawlid Al-Nabi) Sunni Muslims celebrate Muhammad's birthday today.

November 17, 2019: Muhammad's Birthday (Mawlid Al-Nabi) Shia Muslims celebrate Muhammad's birthday on this date.

November 28, 2019: Thanksgiving

Almanack Literature
Beating the Devil
By Mrs. Fairy Huffine

As sometimes happens in families, my father formed a special attachment to his grandmother in his youth. He had lost his own mother when he was only ten years old. This story is one of many she told him, and I have heard him repeat it often.

In 1827 his great-grandparents married, came up from Fairfield County, bought 80 acres just west of Sycamore, cleared the land and built a log cabin and a barn.

Eventually, a larger barn was needed and, with the help of the Wyandot Indians, they erected a large frame building, which had the largest floor space in all of the community.

Now in those days, any new buildings were dedicated with either a three-day religious meeting or a barn dance. In this instance, a religious meeting was planned.

Also, each community had its own rowdies who went to great lengths to add some "excitement" to these gatherings. And this community was no different.

In this instance, these rowdies discovered a wasp's nest at the far end of the orchard. So what better tool, they thought, to use for the "nefarious deed" they had planned to harass the meeting.

Gingerly placing a corncob in the hole of the nest, they proceeded to cut the limb it was on and very carefully carried it down to the barn intending to throw it into the midst of the worshipers.

But just before they arrived at the door, much to their amazement and consternation, the corncob fell out, freeing the mad hornets. Immediately, there was a very intensive flight, each boy fighting for himself.

My husband's great-grandmother always laughed when she arrived at this point, and she always ended her story with: "That was one time the devil got beat at his own game!"

Crime and Punishment
By J. W. Croninger

On the first day of eighth grade, the last year I was in school, we boys discovered a nest of bees in the roof of the girls' outhouse. And so we waited for the five-minute bell to ring at noon, and then we bombed the privy roof just as the teacher and a couple of the older girls got in the door.

As the stones landed, the bees got mad, and some people were stung bad. The man teacher was called out to see, and after that, the boys who were involved were sent to destroy the nest.

We got stung several times and finally had to go in with fire. Well, we got the bees, and the nest too. We also got the girls' outhouse!

The next day, the school board and county superintendent and all who were involved had a meeting outside. And it was settled this way: that the boys who were to blame had to rebuild the backhouse and keep up their grades at the same time without evening or weekend work.

And by the last of October, the job was finished for all the interested parties.

THE ALMANACK HOROSCOPE FOR SAGITTARIUS INTO CAPRICORN IN DECEMBER 2019

Splitting Osage at sunset, half Moon and Aldebaran in the orange sky, temperatures into the teens, and my breath white, I feel like I'm closing in on the rhythm. I feel that everything could be right here in front of me. Limits are clear and distinct this cold Christmas evening. Things mean what they are. I don't need myths, allegories, metaphors. These are the same stars and Moon that shone on Bethlehem. If there is a Jesus, he must be here beside me.

bf

The Gregorian Calendar

S	M	T	W	T	F	S
1	2	3	4	5	6	7
8	9	10	11	12	13	14
15	16	17	18	19	20	21
22	23	24	25	26	27	28
29	30	31				

Taking Stock

At the end of November, I took inventory of what was happening around the yard and in the alley. When I compared my notes with the observations from the same day in previous years, I found that little had changed one year to the next.

My seasonal inventories are like that. They often recreate the past; sometimes they also heighten my awareness of the present and give me a feel for the future. The repetitions of events reinforce a sense of grounding. They bring few surprises or disappointments.

This year, someone asked me if I could give an excuse for my listings, some practical application for writing down the same phenomena year after year. I made up a response on the spur of the moment about the metaphoric quality of all nature, but later I thought about Einstein's statement about insanity as doing the same thing over and over again and expecting different results. And so then I asked myself: What is doing the same thing over and over and expecting the same results, even being excited about the same results?

Fifty years ago, I was always hungry for new sensations. I did everything I could just to do it, just because it was different from what I had done before. These days, I find novelty in repetition. I am glad to find the same plant in the same place blooming at the same time year after year. I am glad to hear the cicadas and the katydids summer after summer.

If each year is generally like the previous year, next year may well be the same as this year. But I am never completely sure, and so I live in a low-grade state of cosmological suspense. There is much at stake, it seems to me, in tracking the recurrence of the most common events; maybe even sanity is at stake.

And there is always compensation enough in doing the experiment one more day. Each time, I am reassured and reaffirmed by the results: I can know at least a portion of the future. It is a place I have visited before. It is familiar ground. It is home.

The Sagittarius-Capricorn Sun

Between December 5 and January 8, is the Season of Solstice (or the Season of Sunstop). This is the time during which the Sun holds within a degree of 23 degrees and 26 minutes, its solstice position, and produces a period of solar stability similar to the one between June 5 and July 8.

Winter solstice occurs at 4:19 a.m. on December 22, and that day the Sun passes from Early Winter's prophetic sign of Sagittarius into Deep Winter's Capricorn, the fulfillment of November's promise. Capricorn is the sign of the year's end and of its beginning, the fulcrum on which longest nights of the year balance and then fall into January and down toward June.

Those born beneath the sign of Capricorn are sometimes said to be ruled by Saturn, the planet associated with time and aging. As the new year of

2019 unfolds, Saturn remains Capricorn's companion, leading that constellation across the day in Sagittarius. It is visible far in the west with Jupiter and Venus near sundown, then disappears until Late Winter, when it reappears to take Capricorn into the morning.

And so Saturn, planet of time, with its companions carries *us,* as well as the Capricorn Sun, from bleak December into shorter nights and brighter days.

We make our lives by the stars and the planets even if we do not believe astrologers. We live by the seasons, are led by the great sky signs from one age to the next, can welcome Capricorn as a gateway to what we will become as its snow turns into pussy willows and periwinkles in Aquarius and then into daffodils and buttercups in Pisces and then into tulips and peonies and iris and mock orange in Taurus in May.

The Silent Cricket Moon
and the Pussy Willow Cracking Moon

By this point in the year, cricket song has quieted deep into the South, and the silence of Early Winter offers a sound of solitude, an absence that opens space for reflection and renewal. The Silent Cricket Moon, like all the Moons between Scorpio and Pisces, can be cruel and challenging, but it also offers a context for personal centering, as well as for finishing the work of the year and preparing for the year ahead.

While crickets sleep, the last leaves fall from woodland asters. Mice and voles find safety in your walls and attic. The stubborn Zelcova, beech and pear leaves finally come down. Crows gather in vast murders to feed in the harvested fields. Hoary goldenrod and brittle great ragweed break in storm gusts. Jerusalem artichokes lean against each other, leaves clutching leaves. Pokeweed stems, hollow and empty, rattle in the wind. Snow and overwintering robins pull off the last honeysuckle berries. Winterberry branches bend to let down their fruit. Bittersweet hulls split away from their branches.

The evergreen foliage of the hardiest herbs and flowers collapses tight against the frozen but nurturing ground, crouches in wait like new seeds through the Moons of Deep Winter, Late Winter and Early Spring.

In spite of the cold and darkness, Lenten roses gradually show their buds, and sap quivers in the maples every thaw. Sandhill cranes travel high toward the Gulf of Mexico. Owls lay out their nests.

And revealing another side of lunar guidance, the Pussy Willow Cracking Moon becomes new just as the Sun begins to rise toward summer. Pussy willows often begin to crack in deeper thaws, and if winter seems too long, pussy willow branches, cut and placed in warm water, forecast March.

If we choose, all these signs and creatures become allies in the darkest days, holding promises and lessons to ponder by the fires we build to guard us from the cold.

December 4: The Silent Cricket Moon enters its second quarter at 1:58 a.m. and reaches apogee (its position farthest from Earth at 11:09 p.m.
The first eight to ten days of December this year should be relatively mild, auguring well for travel.

December 12: The Moon is full at 12:12 a.m.
Lunar phase initiates the season of Early Winter this year, bringing precipitation and hard cold to the nation.

December 18: The Moon reaches perigee, its position closest to Earth at 3:30 p.m. and enters its final quarter at 11:57 p.m.
Lunar perigee negates the warming influence of the waning moon.

December 26: The Pussy Willow Cracking Moon is new at 12:13 a.m.
The New Moon is likely to bring a white Christmas to the north and a chilly passage to the New Year.

The Planets

♃ ♄ ♂ ♀

Mars, rising in Libra before dawn is the Morning Star this month. Jupiter, Venus and Saturn are clustered together in Sagittarius, coming up after sunrise, travelling along the southern horizon during the day and disappearing into the southwest near sunset.

The Stars
Behold Orion rise,
His arms extended measures half the skies.
Manilius

The rising of Orion after 9:00 p.m. continues to be the most dramatic event of an Early Winter evening. The seven sisters, the Pleiades, and the constellation Taurus, precede it.

Due north of Polaris, the Little Dipper hangs in the sky overhead before midnight. North-northeast, the Big Dipper hugs the horizon. Due east, Cancer has just come up. Due south, the gangly formations of Cetus, Fornax and Eridanus wander along the tree line. In the far west, Aquarius pushes Delphinus into the Pacific Ocean.

Past midnight, Orion is fully visible overhead, preceded by Taurus. July's Leo follows Gemini and Cancer across the sky. Regulus, the brightest star of spring, is just starting to rise along the eastern tree line a few hours before dawn.

Many of these stars are relatively easy landmarks for the turning of the Earth, and with just a few them, the time watcher can match what happens in his or her neighborhood with what happens in deep space. One star or constellation is always near others, leading the horoscoper deeper into time. With a simple star chart, one can hopscotch from one marker to another. Naming them is not important, but owning them – making them your own by adopting their movements – is one key to make your own movements in harmony with so many other guideposts of the planet and beyond.

The Shooting Stars

The Geminid meteor shower peaks on December 13-14 near Gemini, with the bright, round Moon interfering somewhat with meteor viewing. The Ursid Meteors fall after midnight at the rate of about five to ten per hour on December 23. The dark Moon will not obscure these shooting stars.

The S.A.D. Stress Index

The shortest days of the year, the increase in cloud cover, and the growing cold all combine with the influence of the Moon to produce high S.A.D. Index readings throughout the month.

This year, the period between full Moon on the 12th, perigee on the 18th and New Moon on the 26th is likely to be one of the most stressful of the entire year.

But the time watcher might fight back and maybe even flourish under the forces that create S.A.D. Herbs brought in from the garden and placed in a south window can be allies against the cold. April-green sprouts growing under lights, blooming amaryllis and paperwhite bulbs, flowering orchids (that often choose to bloom in the year's darkest days), and evergreens can be potent reminders and forecasts of summer and rebirth.

Key for Interpreting the S.A.D. Index:
Totals of 100 to 80: Severe stress
79 to 55: Severe to moderate stress
54 to 40: Moderate stress
39 to 25: Light to moderate stress
24 and below: Light stress

Day	Clouds	Weather	Day	Moon	Totals
December 4:	21	20	24	5	70
December 12:	23	23	25	26	97
December 18:	24	23	25	20	92
December 26:	24	24	25	22	95
December 31:	25	25	25	10	85

Meteorology
Based on Average Arrival of Weather Systems and the Phases of the Moon

Weather history suggests that the cold waves of Early Winter usually cross the Mississippi River on or about December 2, 8, 15, 20, 25 and 29. Snow or rain often occurs prior to the passage of each major front.

It is probable that full Moon on December 12, lunar perigee on December 18 and New Moon on December 26 will bring stronger-than-average storms to the United States. It is likely that the period between December 10 and 28 will be less than optimal for travel, considering the lunar tidal forces.

On the other hand, the odds for a white Christmas improve as the cold fronts that usually cross the continent are strengthened by lunar position.

Weekly Weather Estimates
Week 1

Average highs fall three degrees into the lower 40s this week in the nation's midsection, and typical lows decline to the middle 20s. The first December cold front usually arrives between the 1st and the 3rd, bringing a 40 percent chance of rain or snow on the 2nd and 3rd. The 4th and 5th are dry two years in three; the 6th, however, usually anticipates the second high-pressure system of the month and is wet half the days in my record. Afternoon highs do reach the 60s this week of the year at average elevations along the 40th Parallel, but only 5 to 10 percent of the time. Odds are far better for chilly afternoons in the 30s and 40s and lows well below freezing.

Week 2

This week of the year typically brings the second major cold front of the month between the 8th and the 10th, and the third high-pressure system between the 11th and the 13th. Completely overcast skies dominate 60 percent of the days, and precipitation often occurs as the cold waves approach. Afternoon highs are usually in the 20s or 30s, and this year's full Moon on the 12th will almost certainly bring bitter cold temperatures, preceded by precipitation, the first major snowfall of Early Winter.

Week 3

The Halcyon Days, a traditional two-week period of calm before the turbulence of winter, are supposed to begin in December's third week. According to Greek legend, the halcyon (kingfisher) built its nest on the surface of the ocean and laid its eggs late in the fall. In order to ensure the brood would emerge safely, the bird calmed winds for a week before and after winter solstice.

Be that as it may, this year's third week of December almost always brings in a strong cold wave between the 15th and 20th, and lunar perigee on the 18th will strengthen that cold wave this year.

The coldest December days, those with better than a 35 percent chance of temperatures in the 20s or below, all come at this time of year: the 17th, 18th, 19th, 25th, and 26th. The most bitter day this week in weather history is the 19th, with a 30 percent chance of highs only in the teens. And more below-zero temperatures occur between the 18th and the 26th than on any other December mornings. Precipitation is common throughout the period, with every day this week bringing a 50 percent chance of rain or snow. Double-digit below-zero temperatures are possible between this week and the third week of March.

Week 4

Two major cold waves ordinarily dominate this time of the year. The first front comes in on the 21st or 22nd, and the second arrives between the 23rd and the 26th. Christmas Day is typically the brightest day of the week, bringing a 70 percent chance of Sun. The 28th is the darkest day, with a 70 percent chance of clouds. Snow falls half the time on Christmas Eve and on the two days before New Year's Day. The 26th is typically the coldest day of the week and has almost a 40 percent chance of highs just in the teens or 20s. This year's New Moon on the 26th will make it quite likely that temperatures will not rise above freezing.

Peak Activity Times for Creatures

The following traditional guide to lunar position shows when the Moon is above or below the country, and, therefore, the portion of the day or night during which livestock, people, fish and game are typically the most active and the hungriest.

Activity is likely to increase at New Moon (December 26) and perigee (December 18) and full Moon (December 12), especially as the barometer falls in advance of cold fronts near those dates.

Ordinarily, the Moon's position overhead (above your location) is more powerful than its position below your location.

Date	Above	Below
December: 1– 3:	Afternoons	Midnight to Dawn
December 4 – 11:	Evenings	Mornings
December 12 – 17;	Midnight to Dawn	Afternoons
December 18 – 26:	Mornings	Evenings
December 27– 31:	Afternoons	Midnight to Dawn

Best Lunar Planting Times

Seed bedding plants near the new Pussy Willow Cracking Moon (December 26). Plant the spring garden throughout the South, root crops under the dark second half of the Silent Cricket Moon

(December 13-25), crops that produce their fruit above the ground in the first quarter of the Pussy Willow Cracking Moon (December 26-31).

Calendar of Feast Days and Holidays for Gardeners, Farmers and Homesteaders

December 22 – 30: Hanukkah/Festival of Light This festival lasts eight days and offers many possibilities for marketing.

December 25: Christmas

December 25, 2019 – January 1, 2020: Kwanzaa: Kwanzaa, in Swahili, refers to the first harvest of the year, and this celebration often includes traditional African dishes that contain fresh fruit and vegetables.

Almanack Literature
A Sudden Snowstorm
By Rick Etter

This story is one of my Dad's. For years he wrote snippets of things about growing up on the prairies of North Dakota. This one is about the suddenness and strength of a prairie snowstorm. One nearby family lost three boys that got caught out in it and couldn't find their way home. The fourth survived, but lost a foot and some toes. I recently heard from his family that he passed away around Christmas last year.

***

`Every winter we would get one or more blizzards. These were terrible things to behold unless you were snug in your house. To be caught out on the prairie was almost sure death. It wouldn't have to snow very much, for the wind would churn what snow there was into fine particles not unlike talcum powder. It would choke you if you faced the wind with no cover over your face.

We would use binder twine to run lines from the house to the various out buildings, so we could find our way back if it got too bad. Most people kept a lighted lamp in the window at night in case anyone lost might see it.

On Saturday March 15, 1941, Dad had taken the horses and the enclosed sled that doubled as a school bus into town to pick up supplies. He learned that a snowplow would be clearing the road from town past our farm that evening. It was scheduled to leave town about 6:30 p.m.

Well, we had a truck with an enclosed box on it that we used as a school bus when the roads were open, but this truck had been buried in a snow drift about two miles north of town since an early December blizzard. So Dad, Wally and I were going to take the horses and sled to meet the snowplow at the site of our buried truck. We figured the plow would get there around 8:00 p.m. Since we had no telephone, we had to estimate and hope.

A little before 7:00 p.m., Wally and I went out to the barn to harness the horses. The weather was a balmy 35 degrees and cloudy. We hung the lantern up on a rafter and we were about to get the harness when there was a sudden crash of wind that we thought was going to take the barn down. The barn shuddered and squealed but remained intact.

We immediately looked out the door we had just entered, which was on the east end of the barn, and saw a mass of churning snow. The wind was from the west to northwest. We later learned the velocity of the wind to be between 85 to 100 mph. We couldn't see the house or a light in the house window. Wally took the lantern and we started toward where we figured the house must be located.

I tried to hang on to his coat, but the wind and the choking snow was more than I could handle. The storm smothered the lantern so he dropped it and hung on to me. We missed the house but we bumped against a gatepost. The gate was open, so if we had been a foot to the left we would have passed through the gate and into miles of open country.

We followed the fence back to the garage,

so we knew where we were, but we still couldn't see the house about 20 feet away. We got our bearings and made it to the door where Dad and Mother hauled us in. We had snow under our coats and caps, under our shirts and pants, inside our socks. It was packed between my glasses and my face. No wonder I couldn't see! We were very lucky; since it was so late in the season, we did not have a line from the barn to the house.

All Things Bright and Beautiful
By Sara Beck

Whenever I hear a whip-poor-will call, I am reminded of the summer I was a counselor at a Lutheran leadership camp at the campus of Centre College in Danville, Kentucky.

Every evening we had a vesper service as we gathered on a hillside. A different pastor would lead the devotion, and this particular time, our young pastor, Tim, had the service. His lectern was located in a valley below us in a lovely wooded area. As I looked over the sea of young faces, I felt a great sense of reverence.

Tim prayed, and we sang "All Things Bright and Beautiful." The words went, "All things bright and beautiful, all creatures great and small, all things wise and wonderful, the Lord God made them all," and Tim began his sermonette.

He voiced a few words when a whip-poor-will began his call, "Whip-poor-will! Whip-poor-will!" The call continued, becoming louder and louder.

Tim tried to compete but realized he could not outtalk that bird. He stopped speaking and we listened to the songster with its message.

As I listened to the clear, measured sound in the warm summer air, I was struck in awe. I felt the presence of the Lord.

The bird finished and Tim said, "Amen."

Valediction for the Year

Grounding in just what lies around me,
learning to understand home,
feeling the limits of independence,
the solitude of landscape,
finding enough
in plain observations and events,
embracing the ordinary, expecting nothing more,
accepting this particular passage
of time and location in time,
seeing salvation in the commonplace,
marking the sunlight of solstice on my wall,
counting cracking pussy willows,
measuring the height of winter snowdrops,
asking nothing more than these pure acts,
allowing, opening, watching the finite visions
that contain no transcendence,
no special compensation,
considering the precision of each fragment
that names the exact place of Earth's orbit
and my exact place within it now.

Bill Felker

Bill Felker

Bill Felker has been writing *Poor Will's Almanack* for papers and magazines since 1984, and he has published annual almanacks since 2003. His radio version of *Poor Will* is broadcast weekly on NPR station WYSO and is available on podcast at **www.wyso.org**. Bill has also just published a twelve-volume collection of his nature notes, *A Daybook for the Year in Yellow Springs, Ohio*. A collection of his almanack essays, *Home is the Prime Meridian*, appeared in 2017. All of Bill's books are available on Amazon.

For more information, visit Bill Felker's website at **www.poorwillsalmanack.com.**

Made in the USA
Middletown, DE
12 August 2018